CELEBRITY BRANDING YOU™

By JW Dicks, Esq. & Nick Nanton, Esq.

Published in the United States by D&N Publishing, a division of the Dicks & Nanton Companies, Orlando, FL.

ISBN - 978-0-615-18699-3

---

www.DicksNanton.com
www.CelebrityBrandingYou.com

Cover Photography by Brook Pifer <www.Brook-Pifer.com>
Cover Design by Colin Breaud
Layout by River City Consulting <www.RiverCityConsulting.com>
Edited by Jennifer Dicks Burg & Geoffrey B. Nanton

Printed in the United States of America

10 9 8 7 6 5 4 3 2 1

To Linda, my wife, partner and best friend for 35 years!

To Kristina, Brock and Bowen...the real Celebrities in my life.

CONTENTS

YOUR CELEBRITY BRANDING™ INTRODUCTION

YOUR CELEBRITY BRANDING™ INTRODUCTION

Rule # 1 People Buy People

The central premise of this book and business philosophy is based on a proven fact --

"People Buy People"

Your prospect and your customer would rather make their buying decisions based on you as a person instead of dealing with a company that has no face or personality. This fact has been proven to us time and time again. With more than 50 collective years of running businesses and being entrepreneurs in the real world, we have spent millions of dollars of our own money to develop and prove this fact. We have joint-ventured, coached and consulted with other businesses that are spending hundreds of millions of dollars because they know the powerful business truth that a person or personality attached to your business will make it grow faster and create more money for you.

Many of you, based on your own experiences in the marketplace, immediately understand the importance attached to the business principle of personality-driven business.

Some of you will find this statement to be a surprise at first. Then, once you consider what it means as a potential opportunity for you, your eyes will be opened to a completely new way of marketing and operating your business.

A few of you, many of whom work for "big businesses" that run multi-million dollar ads in slick magazines, won't have any idea of what we are talking about and may even get a little indignant and want to argue this point. You believe in the big, corporate brand and institutional advertising. If this is you, then respectfully, let us suggest that you close the book and take it back to the bookstore. Since you have not read the book, exchange it for a book on the New York Times Best Sellers fiction list and at least enjoy a great read – harsh, but practical.

For the rest of you, including the non-believers who are willing to keep an open mind, we welcome you. You are our people, and we welcome you to a fun way of building your business that will be both rewarding and profitable. Once you "get it," you will experience one of the true unfair advantages left in business today -- a cost-effective way to eliminate your competition. Why? Because the one thing you have going for you that no one can duplicate is YOU. This is important for businesses of all sizes. You can be successful without a "personality," but it is easier to capture market share if you have one, even if the personality is an invented one like McDonald's Ronald McDonald or Burger King's the King (both of which were promoted heavily to counter attack the "up-and-comer" Wendy's who had a real personality in the form of their founder, Dave Thomas, whom everyone still remembers.)

What we are going to do in this book is teach you about the importance of positioning yourself as a Celebrity Brand by becoming the "Celebrity Expert" in your area of expertise and in the market you compete in, be it local or national.

There are five stages of the Celebrity Branding™ process, and each stage has its own benefits.

Stage 1: Finding Your Niche
Stage 2: Creating Your Brand
Stage 3: Developing Your Celebrity Expert Status
Stage 4: Rollout-Expanding Your Celebrity Brand Business
Stage 5: Selling Your Business and Creating "Legacy Dollars"

Each of the five stages of our celebrity-branding process is a distinct and rewarding accomplishment in and of itself. Some of you will not yet have started your first level, and you will require a more compelling story and proof of concept before you begin the process. Some of you have already developed your expert status and are now ready to move on to stage #4 and expand your brand nationally, gaining the enormous profit potential that a national rollout holds. All of you, regardless of your current level, will make more money from your business and be in a personal position to do more good for others if you embrace the strategies we show you. A Celebrity Expert, unlike an unknown expert, has a unique following of fans (enthusiastic customers, clients and prospects). This fan following allows you, as the Celebrity Expert, to focus that group's attention on positive causes and charities that you can help to be more successful in addition to your own business.

If we have grabbed your attention in these first few paragraphs, please open your mind and get ready to experience one breakthrough after another as you embark on the journey we like to call "Celebrity Branding You™."

STAGE 1
Finding Your Niche

1

The Truth About Celebrity Branding™

1

The Truth About Celebrity Branding™

Andy Warhol, the successful American painter, said, "In the future, everyone will get their 15 minutes of fame." In truth, we Americans love our celebrities, and we are always creating new ones. This is becoming even more prevalent in our rapidly increasing "reality" culture of blockbuster television shows like "American Idol" and "Dancing with the Stars." If you can become a celebrity, the world is yours, albeit hopefully for more than 15 minutes. American Idol has even promoted its celebrity judges to cult status and incredible incomes.

Simon Cowell earns a reported annual salary of more than $435 million just for the American and British version of the Idol TV show. That excludes everything he earns on the Idols themselves and their extremely successful recording contracts.

In our marketing and media agency, we have consistently seen the power of celebrity attachment to a product or service, and how it produces an increase in the acceptance and sale of the product or service a company is offering. Over the years, we have come to realize that the simple reason for this is that people would rather "buy people" than the inanimate object of a product. By using a celebrity personality in the form of an expert, it enhances the acceptance and increases the value of the product to the buyer. The buyer becomes more involved with the whole process as they begin to identify with the celebrity and everything they endorse.

Take a moment to think about some of your favorite products that are endorsed by celebrities. You have a positive impression of the product and the celebrity, don't you? The positive impression and loyal feeling is a part of the magic of attaching a celebrity to a product.

Now, shift your vision so you can see YOURSELF as the Celebrity Expert, endorsing your own product or service. This is where the real breakthroughs of taking a proven idea and applying it to your own business to increase its revenue occur. By the way, while we would prefer you to be the Celebrity Expert for your own business, you don't have to be. Many businesses have promoted a pastor, family member or loyal employee to this celebrity status for the business. So, if for some reason you don't desire to be the "front person," don't miss out on the power that personality can bring your business.

How Can You Use This Knowledge to Help Your Product or Service Be More Successful?

Celebrity Branding™ is not about becoming a "fake" celebrity. Celebrity Branding™ is about discovering who you are and your expertise. As an expert in your field,

Celebrity Branding™ allows you to market yourself to your target market in an exciting way that produces a response that your prospect notices and then reacts to in the form of buying your product or service because you are the expert. The buyer believes in you and values your reputation. The more you can personally connect, the more value you create with your buying group.

You can increase your status from "expert," because you are good at what you do, to "Celebrity Expert" when the world learns about you. We accelerate that process for our clients by getting the word out faster. We also help our clients structure their product or service in a way that is welcomed in the marketplace and generates the highest-perceived value.

Who Are You?

To become a celebrity brand, you must discover yourself in a unique and compelling way. You must understand who your client or customer really is and what they need from you. Without understanding this basic core of building your brand, the business structure you build will be hollow and unsustainable. Even after you are successful at building your celebrity brand, you must be flexible to change and adapt to your market. Some of the most successful celebrities of all time, like Cher and Madonna, have been the best at adapting and changing with the times by reinventing themselves while constantly delivering what their target audience wanted. They are successful to a great degree because they never lost focus on their market and always fulfilled the needs and desires of their customers.

While we can't answer the, "Who are you?" question for you. We often help our clients find the answer by looking at the things that we all seem to gloss over when we attempt to look at ourselves objectively. Here are a few questions that will help you figure this out:

- What skills do you have that people find interesting?

- What led you to your current job status? Personal status? Financial status?

- When people refer business to you, what do they tell others about you? (If you don't know the answer to this question, you should ask!)

- Why do your clients continually return to you and your products or services?

- What do you do when providing your product or service that is different than "what everyone else does?"

There are many more questions like this, but you get the idea. We concentrate on the things that most people gloss over and say, "That's no big deal." In fact, we are here to tell you that it is a big deal. You got to this exact point in your life based on a series of events, some memorable, some forgettable, some great and some not so great, but all of those events brought you to this moment in time and have had a lasting effect. No other individual in the world has the exact same story as you, so don't hide who you are and where you come from. That's what makes you unique! The key factor you need to pay attention to when "finding" your story is to allow an objective third party help you weed through the story, pull out the "fluff" and keep the "meat."

We know firsthand how hard it is to be objective about your

own work, so every time we write something, we always turn it over to a team of trusted colleagues, family and friends for their opinion. That is also what we are able to do for our clients; help them be objective.

What is Your Mission?

The next question the world wants answered, once they know who you are is, "What is your mission?" In other words, "How can you help me?" That's really what it all boils down to. What is it that you do that makes life easier, better, more fun or profitable for your customers?

The easiest way to answer this question is by looking at an old marketing phrase, "Tell your prospects about benefits, not features." To understand this concept, let's look at a few examples:

Feature:	**Benefit:**
- Open 24 hours	- Come in when it's convenient for you!
- We offer many loan programs	- We can help you find a loan with the right payment options for you!
- We handle corporate law	- Let us handle your corporate paperwork so you can do what you do best, run your business and make more money.

You can see how telling someone about benefits can help them quickly identify, "What's in it for me?" This breakthrough is necessary for a person to give you the opportunity to earn their business. By telling potential clients about benefits instead of features, you take the guess work out of trying to figure out how your product or service will benefit them; you simply tell them up front!

Who is Your Target Market?

After you learn who you are, you must discover your target market. If you do not understand who your market is, then you will likely go broke trying to reach them. The reason is that in today's business world, marketing is one of the greatest expenses of any business. To keep this cost down, and more money in your pocket, you must be able to target your market as narrowly as possible so that the dollars you allocate to advertising yield the greatest return on investment (ROI).

In selecting your target market, pick a market that you feel passionate about. If you feel passionate about your business, it will be evident to your customer, and they will feel it too. This feeling will, in turn, breed confidence in you and your product or service. Tony Robbins, the great motivational speaker said, "Live your life with passion." Most people simply don't do this. Too often, business people get in a rut and feel trapped in their business. This feeling drains you in many ways and always leads to frustration and unhappiness because you are no longer living with passion.

You are not alone if you have this feeling of being in a rut. We have experienced it too at different times in our careers. We have also known doctors who are tired of working with sick patients and lawyers who cannot stand the thought of practicing law anymore. Often, this is a natural progression of life, but frequently it happens because people choose their area of specialty for the wrong reasons. Maybe it was for money. Maybe it was for a family member who always wanted a doctor in the family. Whatever the reason, time catches up with them. If that is you, then commit yourself to using this time to reinvent yourself and reenergize yourself to live with passion and serve a target market that makes you feel alive and enjoy what you do.

Ask yourself these questions:

- What groups of people use your product or service now?
- Which of these groups do you most enjoy working with?
- Do you feel motivated and energized when you think of providing your product or service to this group of people?

Once you answer these questions, you may well have found your target market. If you have not found the answer, then discuss it with a close friend who knows you best. Sometimes we all have trouble "seeing the forest for the trees," especially when the answer is right under our nose. In this case, there is nothing better than a loyal, objective observer.

What Does Your Market Want or Need?

People react to buying messages for one of two reasons -- to get pleasure or to avoid pain. Think about it. Pretty simple really, these are the two predominant forces in how we react to products or services. We want to buy a car because it gives us pleasure. We go to a doctor to get well and ease pain.

If you are fortunate, your product or service can do both.

A health club, for example, might help you feel better and avoid pain. It can also help you look better and give you pleasure. To be the most successful in that field, you would be wise to help your clients understand what the benefits are, and as they are reaping the benefits, you should reinforce the benefits and the clients' success. Rarely do business owners do this, but they should. If your clients aren't being reinforced in a positive manner, they lose the passion in whatever it is you are providing for them -- just like you would. Have you heard the question, "What have you done for me lately?" Enough said.

Do you reinforce the benefits you offer throughout all of your client communications? In chapters 8 and 9, we will go into the various ways that we suggest you stay in touch with your clients and prospects.

You will find that we believe in using all of the many forms of communication available today, both online and in person. Personal contact does not necessarily mean "face-to-face," although that is often best. Today, more than ever, there are many options that are very close to the feel of personal communication but have a broader reach, such as communications by seminars, teleseminars, webinars and special events.

How Does Your Product or Service Fulfill Your Market's Needs?

The next step in your client development process is to analyze how your service fills the needs of your market. What will it do for them? This answer needs to be conveyed in the form of the specific benefits they will receive.

If your market wants to look younger, then the benefit is that your product can do just that -- make them look younger. Interestingly, the benefit must outweigh the cost (cost is a pain people want to avoid). So, if your product makes them look younger but costs more than what they get in terms of time, money or some other tangible benefit, your sales won't be what you desire. The results (benefits) have to be worth the money invested or, even if you have the most compelling marketing in the world, your customers will not return to do business with you. This is an expensive lesson that no business can afford to learn the hard way.

Many of you likely sell a service that helps people make or save money. Our own book "Celebrity Branding You™" is an example of that type of product. If we ask people to buy a book for $25, and they make $25 using what they learn, will they be happy? Probably not, because the reader has also invested their time in reading the book. What if the information helps the reader to make 10 times the amount invested? Will that increase the satisfaction of their investment? Of course it would, and that is the balance point you have to find. Is the magic number five times invested capital? Ten times? Twenty times? There is no concrete answer, but whatever the number is that tips the scale for your market, once you find it, you will have a group of very happy clients beating a path to your door.

Remember, it does not have to be a monetary return; it can easily be a "quality of life" return. Often a person follows a favorite author from book to book. They buy not only because of the dollar investment return, but the quality of life enjoyment they get while reading the book. A key role in your job of developing your successful product or service is to find the "tipping point" on the balance beam your client walks on to begin to feel the value they receive is worth more than the cost. Then you must continue to put pressure on the value side of the bar.

STAGE 2
Creating Your Brand

2

What Is Your Brand?

2

What Is Your Brand?

Your brand is what makes you uniquely different from everyone else in your target market. Your brand should be readily identifiable so people can quickly say, "That is what I need, and that is the person I want to solve my need!"

5WH

Journalists are taught that the secret formula for writing a compelling article is to answer 5WH -- who, what, when, where, why and how. This is the same with a brand. To have a good brand, you must answer the following questions to convey what you do for your target market:

- Who are you?
- What do you do, and what are the expected results?
- When can you do it, and how long will it take?
- Where do you perform your service?
- Why do you do it?
- How do you accomplish it?

Let us give you an example using our own business.

- **Who:** We are Dicks+Nanton Agency. We use our names in the company name so clients immediately begin to identify with us as people, not just a company. We use our pictures extensively on our Web site and on the cover of this book because we, as people, are identifiers of the brand. In the case of this company, we added the word "agency" because people associate agents with celebrities, and we represent our clients in this fashion. We also have a law firm, and we use our names in it along with the word "law" to convey who we are and what we do: Dicks & Nanton P.A.: The Business Growth Lawyers®. Note that the names we chose are clear, they aren't fancy, but you quickly know who we are and what we do. For the Dicks+Nanton Agency LLC, we selected three words that involve what we uniquely do... turn business people into Celebrity Experts. The brand is unique and has a strong appeal.

- **What do we do, and what are the expected results:** We answer this in our slogan, "Celebrity Branding You™." Also, we often use testimonials in our materials. Third-party testimonials are one of the most powerful tools because interested readers will be more compelled to act based on what someone else says about you than what you say about yourself. Whenever you get the opportunity, let your clients talk about the results you produce.

- **When can you do it, and how long will it take:** Naturally, we aren't always available to immediately start working with a new client. That is one of the reasons we wrote this book. By reading and understanding our philosophy and process, many of you can do it on your own or perhaps just use us to help with a particular stage or process. This reduces the time to get results. If you are a client who is starting from scratch, the process will take longer, but the results are worth the time. The time it takes to reach success is never quick enough, but the one thing we know is that the sooner you begin the sooner you will achieve your goals.

- **Where do we perform our service:** While our services are available nationwide, we have a practical limitation on the number of clients we can personally handle at any particular time, so many of our clients come from surrounding geographic areas. However, thanks to technology, we can serve our clients anywhere.

- **Why we do it:** This is the telling and sharing part of your story. In our case, (even with the wide range in our ages) we both live and breathe business growth and marketing ideas. We are also both lawyers, but law school for us was just a strategy to use so we could answer legal questions for ourselves and understand how to solve business problems that might come up. In fact, Nick tells the story that he always thought he was a little strange in the way he thought about creatively coming up with new business ideas until he met me (Jack) and realized he was not alone on the planet. We both began building and growing our own businesses at a young age, each loving the entrepreneur life -- Nick choosing the entertainment business, and Jack focusing on business development. Now, we choose to combine the skills we have both honed in order to turn business people into celebrities in their niche using proven, proprietary strategies that we have developed through years of practice. We get to "play," be creative and make money in all sorts of different enterprises. It is like Christmas everyday!

- **How do we do what we do:** Many years ago, we discovered that business is formulaic. If you learn the formula for a successful business, your business will grow.

> Please note that we did not say there will not be problems in your business, because there will be. All businesses face problems, and sometimes they cannot be resolved fast enough. We have experienced this personally and have seen some of our clients go through it. What we have learned from experience is that you must adapt to problems by finding creative solutions, and then return to the formula you were following. When you are in the eye of the hurricane, this is not easy to see. Clarity of vision is often a valuable service we give our clients; a view from the outside. Experience is a great teacher, but learning from someone who has been there and can keep you out of harm's way is a better and less painful plan.

"Celebrity Branding You™" is also formulaic. We have created a process that if followed, will return the desired results. There are variations and nuances, but the basic form is the same, and it works each time we follow it. It will work for you too.

These are the answers to our own brand questions. We use the answers in all of our communications with clients and prospects. The more you share with people about yourself and your story, the faster they can make a personal decision about you and whether you will work well together. The ones who like our answers and business philosophy stay with us, and the ones who do not fire themselves before we get the chance. And yes, before you ask, we do fire clients. It is a MUST. Quality of work is extremely important. Working with who you want and the people you can provide the greatest help to because of their openness to your ideas and strategies is what brings excitement and passion to your work. It also frees you to do what you do best, with "real clients." By concentrating on the connected client, you will perform better and the client will be happy because the results are better. This is a business truth that is difficult to see when you are getting started and want to put more food on the table. But the sooner you are able to structure your work around this business philosophy, the more you will be successful, both internally and externally.

3

Putting Your Story Behind Your Brand

3

Putting Your Story Behind Your Brand

Perhaps the single most important element to learn when creating a celebrity brand is to turn your inner personality outward to the public. You must learn to open up and let your market see who you are, warts and all. The more open you are about yourself, the stronger your brand becomes. Naturally, as you expose yourself, you will lose some people who decide you are not the person they want to work with because of their own reasons. This is hard to accept in the beginning because of the feelings we all have toward personal rejection. You have to overcome this feeling and accept the inevitable truth -- you cannot please everyone, and you will be able to help more people in the long run if you focus on the ones who accept you as you are. The more open you are with these people about who you are, the more accepting they will be to your proposition and the stronger your relationship will become. The Celebrity Experts we know who are the best at this have created a network of raving fans who help each other accomplish a great deal more than anyone could do on their own.

Why Do You Do What You Do?

Have you ever asked yourself why? If you haven't, now is a good time to explore that question. If the answer is, "Because this is what I have always done," then it is likely that what you are doing may not make you happy. If you ask yourself the question, and you did not like the answer, then you are not satisfied either.

You don't have to be overjoyed with what you do, nor do you have to be happy all the time about what you do. In fact, everyone is unhappy from time to time because the circumstances make the moment unpleasant. This is different from being happy with what you are doing, and it is likely no one ever told you there was a difference.

Being happy with what you are doing means that your work has meaning for you. Because we spend so much time at it, having meaningful work is important. If you don't enjoy your work, you need to consider why and make the changes necessary to correct it. The more meaningful your work, the more you can use it to help others beyond yourself. In turn, you will find that the results make your work even more meaningful.

What Do People Talk to You About or Complement You on?

The answer to this question generally leads to the answer about what you do best for others. When people come up to you and seek your advice, it shows that they have thought about you and decided you are the person who has the answer they need. They may be right or wrong, but if a pattern develops, then you know how the world views what you do, and maybe who you are.

They have put you into a category, and hopefully, that is where you want to be. If not, then you must discover why people perceive you in that particular light and find out how to alter that perception to be more in line with your beliefs.

How Do You Communicate With Others?

This question isn't intended to address types of communication but the manner in which your communication is received by others. Have you ever received an email and thought that the sender must be really mad, only to find out that wasn't true at all? We all have, and that is the real problem with the email society we live and work in today. We fire off emails without any thought as to how a person may perceive what we are saying. This is why it is important in emails, and other forms of communication, that we are careful about what we are conveying to the recipient. Great harm can be inflicted on a relationship simply because the other person reads "tone" in your email or your voice that wasn't intended.

Remember, in business, you are always on stage. Your customers, clients and prospects are always watching and processing, both consciously and unconsciously, what you say and do, even in your expressions and body language. While this is not a course in salesmanship or the use of body language, we are talking about branding. What you say and what you do is part of that process, and if you aren't conveying what and how you want to be branded, people will brand you themselves. Once they brand you, it is very difficult to get them to change their perception, so analyze your movements and actions carefully.

What is Your Elevator Speech?

Your *elevator speech* is the essence of what you would tell someone about what you do if you stepped into an elevator and they asked. We all have an answer; the issue is whether what we say conveys the right information. Does your answer give the individual a potential benefit to them? If not, they may get out of the elevator without another thought about you as long as they live.

Let's say you were to get into an elevator with us and ask the question, "What do you do?" and we were to say "We're attorneys." Good answer from a speed standpoint, but not so good from a business standpoint. The reason is because the individual across from you is mentally going through the process of pigeon-holing you into one of his brain's filing cabinets. The word attorney is easy to process, and we would be sent to your filing cabinet for this word. Unfortunately, what we don't know is how the word attorney is perceived by this person. If they just got through a messy divorce, the title "attorney" may be well subtitled "jerk," and the relationship we had a chance of starting is ended rather abruptly.

What if instead of attorney we responded, "We Celebrity Brand entrepreneurs and professionals to leverage their time and talents to make the kind of money only movie stars usually make."

Can you imagine the brain working fast to try and find a filing cabinet that holds corresponding information for that category? In most cases, they would not have a file, or the file for "Celebrity" would pop open and the individual would follow up with a question because it needs more input. The follow up is your invitation to provide more information that will interest this person and entice them to see how you can benefit them.

This pigeon-holing process goes on all day with people we meet in elevators and even more often at networking and social events. When it happens, you know the importance of being prepared. Having a statement to tell them what you do will either arouse more interest or convey a strong benefit to the other party, and will make them want to know you more. *Provoking the other person to actually think about what you do is the key.* This first impression can be the invitation to do business with you, or a one way ticket to another conversation.

It is also important that you decide where you want to be pigeon-holed. We have all been taught at one point or another not to pigeon-hole ourselves. This was bad advice at its best. If a potential client doesn't know where to "file you away," then chances are you will be forgotten, and they will never seek you out to do business with you.

In order for people to find a use for your services, you must give them specific benefits and specific ideas about how they can benefit from doing business with you. Let's look at an example in the medical industry. How many brain surgeons do you know that are struggling to pay their rent? We doubt many are. But when someone asks them what they do, they often say, "I am a doctor" or "I am a brain surgeon." By choosing to be pigeon-holed in a narrower classification, they are able to be more readily identified by the person they just met. They also narrow their classification in that individual's mind -- making them easier to recall if they ever need a brain surgeon.

STAGE 3
Developing Your Celebrity Expert Status

4

Building Your Celebrity Expert Image

4

Building Your Celebrity Expert Image

Let's face it, we are all judged by the first impression we give to others. It would be nice if it weren't so, but that would be unrealistic. So, let's just work within the parameters we know to be true.

Since people are going to make a judgment about you when they first meet you, then you must make that impression consistent with your brand. If your brand is formal, then you can't look too casual or people will have an initial impression of incongruence, which leads to disbelief. While you can overcome that first impression, why make it so hard on yourself?

One of our clients likes to be known as "The Blue-Jeans Broker." The reason is because she is in real estate and finds that she spends lots of time touring properties. She also is just a more casual and relaxed person. Consequently, she wears... blue jeans. Sometimes, she dresses things up a notch by wearing a jacket, and she is always neat about her entire appearance. But when you see her, you know who she is and can instantly relate to her and her approach. Her look is congruent.

What Other Ways Can You Reinforce Your Message?

Building your brand image also extends to other ways people see or hear you. One of the first things we recommend to clients is to have a professional photographer take their photo. In our area, we recommend a photographer who is good at shooting covers for bands and album artwork. We recommend her because of the unique look her photographs give to our clients that makes their photos seem "real." Don't ask us how she does it -- that is just her gift. The point is, don't just go down to the little camera booth at the fair and have some snapshots taken (unless that look and feel is congruent with your brand).

Also, don't just go for the "glamour" shots that are heavily promoted from time to time. "Glamour" shots are often so posed that they make you appear unapproachable or like someone who may be trying too hard. Just be who you are and be warm and inviting as though you are talking to your best friend that you just re-connected with after 20 years. Do that, and your pictures will come across well.

Your image also extends to your business cards, Web site and other collateral material. We try and present our clients to their potential client base in as many different media as possible. The reason is because we all have different ways of connecting with people. For instance, think about how you like to learn new information. Is it by listening? Others prefer to read a book because they like to see words and, in some cases, feel the pages. In other people both receptors, visual and auditory, are important. Still others like to just "see" the message. To best reach the largest number of people, you want your message presented in all the different categories. For example, don't just hand out a business card; pass out a CD or DVD as well.

Understanding that people receive information differently helps you see why it is important to have different processes for bringing people to you and showing them what you have to offer. Publishing a book helps you reach certain groups of people. Putting on a seminar conveys your brand to an entirely different set of people who receive your information differently. *Using all forms of media opens the doors to the many different ways people can meet you and become involved with your services.*

5

Building Your Credibility As A Celebrity Expert

5

Building Your Credibility As A Celebrity Expert

When we first talk to clients, many are reluctant to feature themselves as their brand because of internal credibility issues they perceive as a problem. In some cases, it has to do with a lack of a formal education. If this is a concern, you can eliminate it right now because the good news is that very few people care.

At one time, a formal education may have been important. Now, it isn't and many-a-billionaire has dropped out to make his or her fortune, with Bill Gates, the richest man in the world, leading the list. Please don't use this as an excuse to drop out, but don't use it as a crutch either!

If you don't have a formal education, and you feel the need to have some educational credentials, then get certified in your specialty. Certifications are available in almost every field. While you can buy degrees from degree mills that sell them on the Internet, this isn't what we recommend. The degree mill is a misleading method of building your education and if you are found out, and that is usually what happens, you will lose credibility much faster than you gained it. Once lost, it is almost impossible to gain back, and in the age of the Internet, bad information will stay with you forever.

Write a Book

One of the best ways to gain credibility in your field is to write a book related to your expertise. At first, thinking about writing a book is a daunting task. A great way to start is by writing a series of articles on your chosen topic that will later form the chapters for your book. As you write each article, or chapter, you can use it as a "special report" that can be used as a gift or handout.

When we wrote this book, we published many of the chapters as special reports before we completed the entire book. Each chapter was sent to our clients and prospects as we wrote them. Next, we used pieces of the chapters in our blogs and e-zines that we send to our clients. Since these are great ways to get instant information to clients and to stay in touch with them, writing the chapters gave us good reasons to do so.

In addition to using the book chapters you write to stay in touch with your own circle of influence, you can also send out the chapters in the form of articles to article marketers on the Internet. They promote them to other e-zine publishers looking for good material for their clients. More on this later in the book, but for now you should understand that this is an amazing new way to get your material out to the public. You also get a free byline and link to your Web site. This "free advertising" invites people to contact you for more information and check out your services. It is a great symbiotic relationship that everyone profits from. The e-zine or newsletter that you allow to publish your article gets good material, its readers benefit and you get free advertising for your work. Better still, since your article is appearing in someone else's published work, it is essentially a testimonial, and that is one of the best forms of advertising. The publisher is "blessing" your work to their readers, which is a very high form of endorsement that you can't buy.

Testimonials

Testimonials are one of the best ways to build brand credibility. When you say you are great, it is perceived in a certain way, and not always positive. But when others tout you as an expert, it is different. Testimonials are perceived as the highest form of praise and endorsement.

Whatever business you are in, start building testimonials about you and your services as soon as possible. It is really not as hard as it seems because in most cases, all you need to do is ask. Sometimes people do not give testimonials simply because they don't know what to say. This is easily resolved by giving them a quote about you and asking them if it is ok to use. You can also ask them a series of questions. The answers they give are testimonials.

Do not forget to also ask permission to use the testimonials people give you in your materials. Most people have no problem with this and are happy to help, but since some people don't like being exposed to the general public for whatever reason, it is always better to get approval in writing. You do not want to hear from your endorsers later in a law suit. Better to be safe than sorry, as they say!

Using audio and video testimonials can be even stronger than print, particularly on your Web site. Technology is making these audio or video testimonials easier to capture and post on your site. People like to see the people who are recommending you because it helps them make a personal connection. Knowing this means you should try to mix up your testimonials in any marketing piece you produce and have all types of people including men and women of different races and occupations. Use full names and cities of origin if possible because people from the south still believe others from the south, and northwesterners relate better to the people from their part of the country. You may not like this fact, but do not fight it because it's true.

RESOURCE: Check out www.CelebrityBrandingYou.com for our recommended resource for video testimonials.

Newsletter

We think a newsletter is one of the most important forms of communication that you can have with the network of people you are trying to build. In today's high-impact media world, you have to always stay in touch with your network or they will forget about you. We aren't talking about just birthdays and Christmas either. We are talking about at least once a month, and more often if you have good information. The easiest and most effective way to do this in the form of a newsletter.

The newsletter used most frequently today is an online version called an e-zine. We like e-zines and recommend them to all of our clients. On the other hand, we strongly encourage using "snail mail" and sending your newsletter offline as well. This is one of your most important pieces of branding communication, but it is one clients resist because of the cost of printing and mailing it. *Please do not skip this important communication device.* People love to get something they like in the mail. Notice, we said something they like. Sure many people are tired of getting junk mail, but if they like what you are sending them, they start looking for it.

For five years, we have been publishing our own full-color, 82-page, high-gloss magazine on investing and wealth building for one of our companies. Clients love to get it in the mail and some keep it out on their coffee tables. We also know many people use it as "bathroom reading," which they can't do with the online edition we also send. Every once in a while, we are late getting the magazine out and invariably people call to let us know about it. They want the magazine because it has material that is important to them, and that kind of relationship is exactly what you want to build with each of your customers.

Note that we said we send both the offline printed version as well as the online version of our magazine. Like we said earlier, people process differently. We want to offer them information in alternative forms so they can take it in the way they want.

6

Your Client Ladder Of Ascension

6

Your Client Ladder Of Ascension

Your client *ladder of ascension* is the process that allows prospects to become involved with you on different levels with different fees attached. It is extremely important to understand that not all clients will have the same feeling about you and your service at the same time. You have to create different opportunities for them to be involved at different comfort levels. You only give a prospect the option of "yes" or "no" to work with your different levels, and let those who are not fully "sold" on your message work with you in a manner that fits their comfort zone.

In many ways, the client-development process is like dating. Seldom do you ask, "Will you marry me?" the first time you go out with someone. Yes, it happens, and so it is with clients. Sometimes they meet you and want every service you have to offer as soon as possible. Most, however, prefer to be courted. These prospects want to know that you really are who you appear to be, and that you aren't trying to hoodwink them the way so many others try to do. Today's prospects are often more skeptical than ever because they are constantly being bombarded with marketing messages. Fear of being taken advantage of is strong. Media clutter and fear must be overcome, and the best way to do that for most people is in baby steps.

To allow for the courting process, you must have a system to introduce clients to you and your product or service in steps. This system should give them opportunities to (1) talk and relate to you, (2) buy a basic product or service that you have to offer (similar to going on the first date), (3) test your products to see if they do what you say and (4) buy other products or services that you offer. Also like dating, the process can end quickly. To avoid this and continue to build the relationship, you must make sure that whatever your ladder of ascension looks like, you must make each and every person feel important, no matter what product or service they bought, whether it is the cheapest or the most expensive.

In a service business like ours, you should have several potential points of entry. The lowest on the ladder of ascension in our case would be to receive a free e-zine or article. The highest might be the sale of a company. The ladder would work like this:

- Free e-zine or free offer for a product/service
- Purchase a book
- Purchase an audio or video course
- Attend a conference
- Become a Coaching/Mastermind Client
- Become a Celebrity-Branding Client
- Become a National-Rollout Client
- Sale of business or "roll-up"

The ladder works because a client could contact us at any point of the process, and we would be happy to work with them. While, clearly, some of the levels are more profitable to us than others, we must treat all of our clients with the same level of courtesy and respect, because some of them may need to go through the process step-by-step.

Additionally, while some people who come into the ladder of services may not go all the way through the ascension process, they may refer someone who does. This is another reason you have entry options. A reader of our book might not want the Celebrity Branding™ service but might think it perfect for their partner or a family member. If we didn't offer alternative services, that person may not understand enough about what we do for them to have the confidence to make a referral.

7

The Dynamic Web Site: Your Keystone Branding Strategy

7

The Dynamic Web Site: Your Keystone Branding Strategy

The keystone in building is the stone on which the foundation and all of the construction rests. Remove the keystone, and the foundation is unstable.

In today's business environment, the keystone is your Web site and Internet strategy. Please note, we said two things -- your Web site AND Internet strategy. Together we call these tools your Online Marketing Platform™. Indeed, having one without the other is futile. While putting up a Web site is helpful, you must understand what you want to get out of it. This is where most businesses fail. They believe having a Web site is all they need, and they are surprised when it doesn't generate the business they thought it would.

The Online Marketplace: The Future of Your Business Today

Do you have any employees who work 24 hours a day, seven days a week, 365 days a year, can answer every question thrown at them, give prospects exactly the information they are looking for, collect credit cards, deliver products when a prospect is ready to buy, take down important questions from potential clients and deliver them to you when you are ready to receive them?

We didn't think so. But the right kind of online presence can do exactly that, not to mention a whole slew of other things. But not just any Web site can accomplish these functions, what you must have is an Online Marketing Platform™.

If you don't have the right kind of Web site, you are losing out on an infinite amount of potential customers. It's kind of like sitting on the side of a river, with your rod lying on the ground next to you. If you don't put it in the water, you're never going to catch a fish.

The purpose of this chapter is to open your eyes to what the right Web site can do for your business and how to go about building this powerful business tool that can go to work for you 24 hours a day, seven days a week, 365 days a year.

What is an Online Marketing Platform™?

An Online Marketing Platform™ (OMP) is a key element to your business because it features the right set of tools to attract prospects, give them just enough information to make them beg for more and convinces them to leave you with their email address (their most valuable commodity, besides a working credit card number, in the online world) so you can contact them in order to turn them into a customer.

The 12 Success Elements Every Web Site Needs

OMP's come in many shapes and size but have a consistent objective. They attract target prospects, project your brand and capture the prospect as a potential client or customer. This is important because it is all about the customer. *Your objective is to capture the potential customer so you can market to them forever.* The customer is the real value of a business. However, until you get their name and contact information, you cannot establish a lasting relationship.

The core elements of an OMP are as follows:

1. Newsletter Sign Up Form
2. Blog's
3. Articles
4. Bonus Items
5. Latest News
6. Testimonials
7. Contact Information
8. Calls to Action
9. Information About Your Business
10. Partner Links
11. Answers to Frequently Asked Questions
12. eCcommerce Capability

Let's discuss them one by one:

1. Newsletter sign-up form

If you aren't attempting to collect at least the email address of every potential client who comes to your Web site, then you are missing one of the greatest prospecting tools of our time.

Let's face it, the reality is that most people are too lazy to really figure out what they need, so they use today's most common research method, search engines, to try to find solutions to their problems. Odds are that even if you have exactly the solution they are looking for, they aren't going to be ready to hire you or buy your products the moment they land on your page.

Think about the way you browse the Internet. If you are like the average surfer, you look at one site, then move onto another and so on until you either find the perfect solution quickly (which is rare) or you get distracted by something else and decide to come back later to find your solution. And when you sit back down to find your solution, how often do you end up at the same sites you stumbled upon the first couple of times you searched for solutions? Not many. *The businesses you visited before lost the opportunity to keep you.*

Why leave this to chance? What you need is a method of collecting the email address of every person who lands on your Web site. The easiest way to do this is with a newsletter sign up form. It often looks like this:

Join Our Mailing List!

Full Name: [   ]

Email: [   ]

CLICK HERE TO REGISTER NOW!

The purpose of capturing your clients email address is to establish a means of contacting them. It would be nice to get all their information at this point, but it isn't going to happen. In fact, you're probably going to have to entice them with a benefit to even get their email address. A free newsletter is one way. Another way is to offer a special report, white paper, free trial or discount, in exchange for their email address.

This initial prospecting strategy allows you to use your Web site as a unique filtering device. As we all know, not everyone is immediately ready for your service. Potential prospects can visit your site, gather information about you and mentally file it away for a future time when they need your service. Once you have their contact information, you can continue to market to them using a soft-sell, drip-marketing system that "automatically" stays in touch with prospects with a constant supply of information they want and need. While you are supplying valuable and interesting information to your prospects, you are also creating a database of future clients who are learning about you over time and are more likely to turn to you when they need your product or service in the future.

Because of this powerful contact system, your Web site should be devoted to creating extraordinary value for the people who visit. We are constantly amazed by the number of major corporations that "miss the boat" on their Web site and use it more as an institutional business card about their company. Bad thinking. *Use your Web site to be personal with everyone who visits.* Make the time that prospects spend on your site a valuable experience. Give them an opportunity to do some business with you, even if it is nothing more than giving you their name and email address in return for a special report or e-newsletter you offer.

2. Blogs

Many of you know what a blog is, but for those who don't, it is a dedicated place for you to communicate with your customers and prospects.

A blog (short for a web log) is an online journal or diary that allows you to write and post information or ideas you feel will be of interest to your readers.

So, how can your blog help you grow your business? Great question. To understand the answer you have to know a bit about how search engines work.

Search engines like Google, Yahoo, MSN and all the others use what they call "spiders." Spiders are software programs that "crawl" the Internet looking for new content and rank it based on this content and its relevance to a certain topic. This is all done by some very complex math, but the important thing you need to know is that if you write often and/or discuss topics that are often searched online (i.e. topics in the news), the search engines will consider your site "relevant." If you also include "key words" (popular search terms) in your content that you know potential customers are searching for, there is a much better chance that they will actually find you when they type those words in a search engine. The more often you blog, the greater likelihood you will appear higher on a page when someone conducts a search using key words related to your product or service.

Our three principles of blogging for search engines are:

1. Write Often
2. Write Relevant
3. Write Using Key Words

What makes a good blog?

The only thing that really matters is the opinion of the audience you are trying to reach. Here are a few tips that will help you develop your blog to generate business.

1) **Know who you are writing for.** If your audience is 13-year-olds, writing about retiring next year probably isn't going to get you a lot of return visitors. Writing about becoming a teenager, the best car to get when you turn 16 and how to attract the opposite sex will probably make you pretty popular.

2) **Keep it short and to the point.** Approximately 100-300 words is all most people have the time to read. Remember, in the online world, people are looking for actionable answers -- not novels (or they would go to a bookstore). So, keep your blogs short and to-the-point. Over time, this will build a great deal of credibility with your readers.

3) **Write actionable content.** "How Tos" and "Top 10" lists are great. It gives your readers action steps that they can take and use in their everyday lives. Think about ways to use this type of content to point out how you are different from your competitors.

4) **Don't be afraid to tell some of your secrets.** People love to hear about how to make something happen, and then they love to pay someone else to do it. Let's be honest, even if someone just told us how to edit the code on our Web site to make it stick out like neon lights in a search engine, that doesn't mean we want to do it ourselves. Just give us a way to contact and hire you. After all, you just showed us you are the expert.

5) **Allow comments.** Consider allowing people to post comments about your blogs. In fact, you should be the first one to post a comment after each blog. Pose a question or comment to simply get a discussion started.

If visitors are interacting and writing comments about your blog, they are actually adding relevant content that the search engines are going to like.

3. Articles

Articles work the same way as blogs in regard to driving up the relevancy of your Web site in search engines. The online game is content driven, so the more relevant content you have on a subject; the more likely you are to get traffic to your site. Articles allow you to show your expertise in a manner that is easily digestible to your visitors. The key to these articles, similar to blogs but slightly longer, is to keep them short and actionable. Give your potential clients information that they can use, and they will trust you even more -- getting you one step closer to earning their business.

Articles are usually a bit longer than blogs, but they don't have to be. Tell what you need to, but keep it slim. Remember, you are trying to build credibility as well, so try to keep your headline relevant to the context of your article. You should also keep your sales pitch to a minimum in your article. *There's nothing worse than looking for good information on a topic, getting three sentences into an article and getting a blatant sales pitch.* Articles are meant to be informative, so try to leave the sales pitch out. At the end of your articles, consider adding a section like this:

To get more information or to review other free special reports, visit www.DicksNantonAgency.com. JW Dicks, Esq. and Nick Nanton, Esq. founders of Dicks + Nanton Agency LLC, publish the "Celebrity Branding You™" e-zine monthly covering topics that every person looking to build their business needs to know. If you're ready to take your business

to the next level, get more FREE info now at www. DicksNantonAgency.com.

This text can serve as your sales pitch. By adding in a link to your Web site, if you publish the article on any additional Web sites, you create additional inbound links to your site. This is another search engine optimizing strategy that helps bring traffic to your Web site.

In chapter 9, we will show you how you can syndicate your articles to become an instant Celebrity Expert and drive more targeted traffic to your Web site.

4. Bonus items

Everyone likes something for free. So, give the people what they want! By using bonus items, you can lure even more visitors to leave their email address with you. Some of the most commonly used bonus tactics are:

1) Give visitors access to special reports that contain more detailed information than what is posted on your Web site. (A great headline can work wonders for getting people to take action.)

2) Give away prizes. Who wouldn't sign up for a free iPod?*

3) Give visitors a free trial of your product, or hold a drawing that gives one winner your product or service for free.*

*Make sure you check your state laws on drawings and giveaways. States usually require a few things in order not to cross the line into the world of "gambling" or "games of chance."

5. Latest News

This is an easy concept, but most people miss it. So, you may want to read this part twice.

People do not know what you are doing unless you tell them.

It's as simple as that. Did you land a big contract? Did your business just celebrate its 20th anniversary? Are you under new management? Are you opening a new location? Are you involved in a charitable cause?

These are just a few of the questions that most of your clients would love to know. If they don't know, you simply aren't effectively communicating the answers. Having a "latest news" section on your Web site allows you to post such items in a manner that makes them look like news, not like you're bragging about yourself. Write in the third person for these posts, and they will really keep your clients in the loop.

TIP: When you announce news that involves other parties, mention them by name. Using other parties' names creates a doubly effective post because the search engines will now also pick up your site when surfers are looking for information about the other parties mentioned.

6. Testimonials

We already paid homage to testimonials in chapter 6, but in our opinion you can never talk about testimonials too much. Testimonials are amazingly powerful, yet often forgotten. There is no more powerful statement about your business than a third-party testimonial. Every person you do business with comes to you for a reason. Maybe you're the best at customer support, maybe you have the most convenient location or maybe your venue is clean. Whatever the case, there is a reason.

You are missing a huge opportunity to learn more about your business and attract new clients if you don't ask your clients why they come to you. Ask your clients for the reasons, and they will give them to you. Have them write the reasons down or record them when they are talking, then you can use them on your Web site (and everything else) to help convince new clients that other people love doing business with you, so they probably will too. There is no such thing as too many testimonials!

Think about it, if you walk into a business and see hundreds of thank you letters from clients posted all over the walls, you are going to ask yourself one question, "What have I been missing?" Because if all of those people are happy enough to write letters, then you're probably in the right place.

Testimonials can be in many forms. The best format is video, just behind that is recorded audio with a photo and last, but definitely still miles ahead of having nothing, are written testimonials with or without a photo. The Internet is a mixed medium, so take your pick!

You have to be conscious of making sure your testimonials don't look manufactured and that they are believable. The best way to do this is to credentialize the individuals who give you testimonials. Here is a common format for doing so:

"Testimonial Here..." – First and Last Name, Title, Company or Organization – City, State, www.Website.com.

If you'd like to see our tool of choice for creating video

testimonials for your Web site, log on to the resources section of www.CelebrityBrandingYou.com. We will show you a tool that is by far the easiest tool you can use to add video to your site in "less than 87 seconds."

7. Contact information

You MUST make it easy for visitors to reach you and ask for more information. Make sure you have at least a phone number (800 numbers are best) and email address on every page. Studies show that putting these at the top of your Web site all the way to the right side is most effective.

You will also find that some visitors want to type a question to you and don't really know how to use email well, so don't miss out on getting the business of these folks too. You can cater to these visitors by creating a web form that they can fill out and submit to you without needing to use email. Here is a common format for a "contact us" form:

Name:	
Email:	
Phone Number:	
Comments/Questions:	

CLICK HERE TO SUBMIT!

Tie all of the forms you have on your Web site to your database system, because some people will email you a question and never sign up for your mailing list. You don't want to forget about these people or lose their information, so add them to your database automatically. For our database system of choice, log onto the resources section of www.CelebrityBrandingYou.com.

8. Calls to action

Most people who come to your Web site don't know what exactly they should do, so don't miss out on the opportunity to tell them. You can do this by using what is commonly known in the marketing world as a "call to action."

Here are a few examples of calls to action:

- Click here for a 50% discount!
- To get the best information in your inbox every month sign up now!
- Buy now and receive FREE shipping!

You get the picture, but the key is to have compelling headlines that will make your visitors take action now! If you want them to buy something, tell them. Most people will usually listen, if you give them a good reason to do what you say.

9. Information about your business

One of the biggest fears for most people who are thinking about doing business with you online is that they don't know you personally, and they want to make sure you aren't trying to scam them. The best way to remove this fear from site visitors is to literally take it back to elementary basics, as in "show and tell." By this I mean you should both show and tell visitors who you are.

Tell them about your company:

a. When it was founded
b. Where you are located
c. Who the principals are

d. Who the core management team is
e. Who some of your customers are
f. What you do

Show them pictures of:

a. Big events that you have attended (trade shows, symposiums, seminars)
b. Your office
c. Your products
d. Key executives
e. Recreational activities and events with clients and staff members

These are just a few examples. Remember to treat them as if they were walking into your office for the first time. What do you have in your lobby that tells clients who you are? What about in your office? Do you have pictures on your desk? Do you have diplomas on the wall?

Remember, clients on the Internet cannot see these things, so try to show them in the best way you can. Make sure they know that you are real people and that will clear a huge hurdle in getting business in the online world.

10. Partner links

We all use search engines to make our online quests easier. And the reason we do is because they are good at what they do, and we have come to know and to trust the results of the search engines.

In order to keep the search engines working, and to keep their customers happy, search engine companies do a lot of work behind the scenes to make sure the results they deliver are valuable and accurate. In order to do so, they use complex mathematical equations, called algorithms, that are highly confidential and take all sorts of factors into account, assign a value to each factor and spit out a ranking that displays Web sites in order of relevance.

One of the really important factors that the search engines look at is if your site is a destination online for the niche that you serve. Since it would be impossible for the algorithm to do it any other way, what search engines do is scour the Internet to see how many sites link back to yours. *The presumption is: the more people who link to your site, the more valuable your information is.*

Search engines are not stupid, and the trick of posting your site on "link farms," sites you can pay to link back to your site has been discovered. In most cases this no longer works to boost your ranking. In fact, it can be seen as "link spamming" and can actually hurt your ranking.

What you are looking for in a link partner are Web sites that have something to do with the business you are in. Then try to get them to link back to you.

How do you do this?

We have found that the easiest way is to offer to trade links. All you have to do is look for Web sites that are the most respected in your industry and email the webmaster to ask if they'd like to swap links. You will agree to post a link to their site, if they will post a link to yours. Once they agree, just post it on a page on your Web site that features all of your "preferred partners," which is really just a nice page with lots of links to other sites.

If you'd like to try a more advanced strategy, type a key word into Google that you would like your site to have a high ranking and look at the first page of results. Copy and paste the domain names of the sites on the first page of Google's search results. Then for each of the domains you listed, type in Google's search bar:

Link: www.InsertDomainNameHere.com

This will allow you to see what other Web sites are linking to each of the sites listed on the first search page. Then you can email those sites and ask them if they would be interested in swapping links with you.

This one simple tip can get you a lot of traffic and a much higher web rank.

11. Answers to Frequently Asked Questions (objections)

In the world of sales, we all have to deal with "objections." Simply put, objections are reasons people might not do business with you.

Here are a couple of common objections:

1. Price is too high/low
2. Quality isn't good enough
3. Location is too far away

As you might have guessed, there are countless other objections. Often, the reason consumers don't buy products and services is that they make up their own answers to questions because no one is there to answer them, especially online!

So, what can you do to avoid this? Answer these questions

and other questions that your customers often ask. To do this, we create a "Frequently Asked Questions" page (an FAQ page as it is known in the online world), and we list the common questions that our clients have and the answers.

This strategy isn't used nearly enough in the online world or in the offline world for that matter. Just a few simple questions and answers can remove a lot of fear from a potential buyer and get them one step closer to becoming a client.

When someone signs up for your mailing list, don't assume they have read all of the content on your site. A great strategy is to email your list of FAQs to the potential client. You can email them one at a time or email them an entire list. We have found that this can greatly increase your response rate!

12. eCommerce capability

Every year, consumers are getting more comfortable buying online. Your site should give them that opportunity. It doesn't always seem like a great fit for every business, but there are few businesses that would not benefit from allowing some sort of e-commerce activity on their site. After all, it's one of the only ways to make money while you sleep. We can assure you that the first time you wake up and find unexpected funds in your bank account, you will have a big smile on your face…trust us!

Advanced strategy: use multiple web sites

What Type of Web Site Do You Need?

This question confuses people who don't understand that there are many different types of Web sites with different purposes. Most people only have one Web site. Unfortunately, having only one Web site reduces your opportunity to present your story to different people in different ways. Not using the right type of Web site to convey your story is also a waste of time.

Clearly, everyone needs a main Web site as the hub of their business. You should also consider an additional site for each target market that you serve or even each product or service that you offer. By having more than one Web site, people can access and get the specific information they need instantly, without being confused by things that aren't relevant to their needs. While at any of your sites, you can always take the opportunity to lead them to your main site where they can get more information about your expanded array of products or services.

We discussed blogs earlier in this chapter. You can make your blog part of your site, but you can also leave it to stand on its own (i.e. allow visitors to access it at the domain www.YOURSITEHEREblog.com. This is another example of the power in multiple sites. People who find your blog through your promotional efforts get instant gratification of what they were looking for, and, based on your blog's design, you can let them know there is more information available on your main site and have a quick link that takes them there.

There are many other ways to use multiple Web sites to increase your exposure. Think about having a dedicated Web site with a sales letter for each specific product or service you offer. It's a great thought isn't it? And… YES, it works.

For a start, concentrate on your main site. When it's completed, remember to be open to new opportunities to expand on the Web.

8

Your Online Marketing Platform™: Design, Build, Promote, Monitor And Optimize

8

Your Online Marketing Platform™: Design, Build, Promote, Monitor And Optimize

Now that you know what makes a great Web site, let's talk about a few more important steps; how to have a Web site built, how to promote it and how to use it to create revenue.

Phase I: Design & Build

Construction

Much like building a house, there are many decisions to make when building your Web site. To keep the analogy rolling, in many cases you can act as the general contractor and hire subcontractors to do the heavy lifting, or hire someone to be the general contractor for you, and they can handle everything.

If you hire an individual or a firm to handle everything, make sure you create a list of deliverables and time limits for completion. Look at samples of past work to see if you like their finished product. Never pay all of the money for the project up front and tie compensation to performance -- especially when it comes to meeting deadlines.

If you are brave enough to oversee the entire process, and just subcontract with others to get the job done, here are some practical tips we have learned that will save you some time, money and headaches.

Planning... or Lack Thereof

The first step in having a Web site built is to plan for what you think you are going to need. Gather samples of other sites that you like so you can see how they are laid out, the style of design that you like, what some of the best sites are doing right and what some of the worst sites are doing wrong.

Once you have done this, you can start creating a content outline. Start by numbering a piece of paper and writing down your key Web pages, the ones that will be the hubs of your site. For example you might have:

1. About us
2. Testimonials
3. Contact us

You get the idea. As you continue, you can break down each page to show what will be included on it. As another example:

1. About us

    a. Picture of key personnel
    b. Two to three testimonials
    c. Paragraph about what you do
    d. Links to three of your best selling products

Continue to do this for the rest of the site. Once you have a good outline, you can start to get some idea of what this site is going to cost. Without the outline, no designer can give you a realistic quote because all Web sites are not created equal! Which leads us to our next point…

All Web Designers Are Not Created Equal!

There are many factors to be taken into account when hiring a web designer. We hate to be stereotypical, but web designers can be very artsy, very techy or both. When you get web designers to quote your project, pay attention to how they treat you. If they are exceptionally hard to get in contact with, think about how you will feel when they have a significant amount of your money as a deposit and you still can't get a hold of them, or when they are a week late on your deadline and you can't get them to return your calls.

If a designer treats you in a way that you aren't quite sure of before you even give them any of your hard earned money -- RUN. This is a bad sign!

A good web designer should be professional, have a good eye for art and should be able to advise you on the smartest way to build your Web site in order for it to accomplish your goals. Don't let them talk you out of what you want! Many designers are horrible business people and will try to put form over function. Remember, you are the one who knows your business. Don't let a designer try to pitch you on something that you know won't work. If it doesn't work for you in the offline world, there is a great chance it won't work for you in the online world.

One great place to find web designers is Elance www.elance.com. It's kind of like an eBay for subcontractors except that you post a job, they bid on it and then you choose the one that you want to work with and award them the job. Once again, use common sense, check their portfolio, check their feedback from previous customers and always use Elance's payment method (because it protects you from indiscriminate people who are just trying to take advantage of you). There are many other places that you can find good web designers, not the least of which is a referral from someone that you know who has a Web site that works (meaning it generates business). Another site that has given us great results is www.craigslist.com. Just remember, don't throw your commonsense out the window!

Considerations When Having Your Site Designed

Design

Your design should be in keeping with your brand and should be an extension of your company in the offline world. Prepare a list of parameters for your designer that outlines the colors you are willing to use as well as colors you hate. Describe your ideal customer and include samples of sites you do and don't like. This will give your designer a good starting point.

Navigation

While many people don't think much about how visitors are going to get around their site, this can be a fatal flaw in converting visitors to clients. While animation and drop down menus look neat, remember that not all web browsing software programs are created equal. This means there will be users who do not have the latest technology and thus may not be able to view your high-tech menu. While getting fancy can be fun, you want to make sure that a visitor never has to "figure out" how to browse your site. If they have to think too hard, they will likely just leave your site for one that isn't so hard to use.

Look at some of the biggest money making sites online: Amazon.com, Ebay.com, Google.com. Notice that they are all extremely easy to navigate. There's a reason for this!

Search engine optimization (SEO) considerations

Three tips that will make you look like a web pro and keep your web designer on his toes!

While we could write a series of books on SEO alone, and many of the advanced strategies are beyond the scope of this book, a little knowledge in this field goes a long way. SEO is one of your key online marketing tools. As a matter of fact, here's a great test for any web designer you are thinking about hiring. Ask them their thoughts on "SEO." If they fumble, or worse yet don't even know what you're talking about… RUN.

The way your site is designed can help or hurt the way your site is viewed by search engines. Here are just a few SEO rules that you need to make sure your designer adheres to:

1. Use text as often as possible.

There are several uniform fonts that all web browsers can display. If you use a font outside this realm, your designer will have to create an image using the fancy font and it will display as an image on your Web site. The problem here is that search engines cannot read images, and this will put your site at a disadvantage for online marketing.

2. When you do use images, use Alt Tags.

A picture is worth a thousand words. Don't think that we are discouraging the use of images. We use them on all of our sites. When you use an image, there is a tool called an "alt tag" that allows you to describe the image. Make sure you use these; it's like giving the search engines a helping hand to decipher what's on your site. The more you try to help search engines, the more relevancy they will give your site and the better your ranking will be.

3. Give each web page within your site a different title.

Tell the search engines what each page is about by giving each page a unique title that contains the main key words and phrases that address what is contained on the page. Putting keywords (but not too many!) within the title of your pages is a great SEO technique that will help your Web site climb up the rankings. It will also allow your visitors to remember exactly what your page is all about when they bookmark your site or save it to their "favorites."

Phase II: Promoting Your Web site

Five Traffic Generating Tips That Will Have New Potential Clients Beating Down Your Virtual Door

The majority of Web sites fail because they only complete Phase I. They build a Web site believing that people will now beat a path to their door. Unfortunately, this isn't the case. If you have ever had a Web site, you probably know what we mean. Your site must now be promoted in order to get the results you want. The more it is promoted, the more "hits" you get. The more hits you get, the more interest that is generated in the site from all sources -- individuals to search engines. Creating a buzz about you or your business is the most important phase because without it everything you did in Phase I is wasted.

1. Key Words

Key words are what your client is looking for. If they are looking for anti-aging medicine, their key words might be: anti-aging, feel younger, look younger, young again, etc. If you don't know what your clients are looking for, this is a question you need to answer because it is the foundation for promoting your site.

In order to get an idea of what your clients are looking for, use Google's keyword tool at: https://adwords.google.com/select/KeywordToolExternal. All you have to do is type in several of the names of your products or services, and it will give you suggestions.

Another great tool is Wordtracker, www.wordtracker.com. Wordtracker can help you see how many times a particular word is searched. It actually gives you a rating you can use to see if you should spend time trying to promote a keyword, or if you should look for something else because the market for that word is too cluttered.

Using these tools, you can take a look at what your clients might be typing and then find the best combinations of words that will attract new clients. Similar to fishing in a river with the wrong bait, the wrong key words can lead to a dry harvest.

2. Pay-Per-Click (PPC) Advertising

Pay per click is considered by many to be one of the most effective forms of advertising because you pay only for people who come to your site from the ad you place. The key words we mentioned above are often great pay-per-click words as well, but there are many more that you can also test.

Popular search engines like Google, Yahoo and MSN use pay-per-click ads for their top results on their search pages. Quite often, the pay-per-click ads are placed at the top of the search page and down the right side.

The way it works is through an auction system. The words that are in highest demand, command the highest prices. The amount you bid determines your placement on the search pages. You want to try to make sure you show up on at least the first page of the search because most people never even get to the second page of search results.

Most search engines that sell pay per click words will allow you to set a bid for the keywords you are interested in and a daily budget that you don't want to go over. There is only one way to see what works, test, test and test some more. Don't be afraid to spend some money here, but monitor your spending. We can tell you many horror stories of both novice and experienced pay-per-click advertisers who have blown more money than you'd like to know on keywords that didn't work. Don't do this to yourself until you fully understand the process! Start out with low limits and adjust them as you go. For the most part, web traffic follows patterns. So, don't worry about getting all of the traffic today. In all but the most unusual of circumstances, we can assure you it will be there tomorrow!

3. Blog Syndication

We talked about blogs earlier in the book, but one of the best tools for promoting your business and your celebrity-expert status is to syndicate your blog. You can use many tools to do this, but one of the easiest to use is www.feedburner.com.

What happens when you syndicate your blog is that you turn it into what is called an RSS (Really Simple Syndication) feed that users can plug into their RSS reader. This way they can keep the newest content that you write flowing through their RSS reader without constantly having to come back to your site on a daily basis (which most people simply aren't willing to do). It takes some work to gain this sort of trust from your readers, so don't be discouraged if getting RSS subscribers doesn't happen overnight.

If you don't have an RSS reader, we recommend www.iGoogle.com. It allows you to organize all kinds of information, including RSS feeds. It's like having all of your favorite newspapers in front of you at one time, and you can keep them up-to-date without having to visit a bunch of Web sites. Try it out, and then you'll understand why syndicating your blog is so important. It makes it very easy for those who want to keep up with your latest posts.

4. Article Marketing

As you are well-aware by now, one of the key strategies in creating your celebrity-expert status is creating actionable content that your clients can read. We advocate doing this in the form of blogs and articles. You can post both to your site, and, as discussed previously, you can syndicate your blogs. Now, we're going to tell you how you can syndicate your articles too. This is often referred to as article marketing.

Article marketing isn't the same as blog syndication because when you syndicate your article, instead of creating an RSS feed that people can subscribe to, your article is actually published on multiple Web sites. What makes this really valuable is the "about the author" section of the article. By including a link to your Web site in this section, wherever it is posted you will get an inbound link to your Web site, which, as we discussed earlier, is a great tool in boosting your search engine rankings.

Here is a sample of what we mean:

WANT TO REPUBLISH THIS ARTICLE? You can, as long as you include this blurb with it: JW Dicks, Esq. and Nick Nanton, Esq., attorneys by trade and entrepreneurs by choice, are the one consistent force for their clients in the rapidly changing business world. The Dicks + Nanton Agency LLC represents entrepreneurs, executives and Celebrity Experts to maximize exposure and uncover hidden opportunities to increase income and growth in the business. The Dicks + Nanton Agency LLC publishes the "Celebrity Branding You™" e-zine covering topics that every business professional needs to maximize their income potential. Get more FREE tips that will allow you to make more money and work less NOW at www.DicksNantonAgency.com.

Some Web sites allow you to post your article on their site for free, and others charge a fee to submit your article to hundreds of Web sites automatically. They are both great services, and you should use them based on your needs.

Here is a list of a few of our favorite article syndication sites:

- www.ezinearticles.com
- www.isnare.com
- www.articlemarketer.com
- www.submityourarticle.com

To find more article syndication resources, visit the resources section of www.CelebrityBrandingYou.com.

5. Online PR and Press Releases

No one knows what you're up to if you don't tell them. While this sounds like a ridiculously obvious statement in your personal life, most businesses don't adhere to such common sense.

So, how do you do this? Press releases are one of our favorite ways. You can write them relatively easily yourself or hire someone to write them for you.

Now, we'll let you in on a big secret: All of the official sounding press releases that talk about a company winning an award or doing something great, are written by or under the supervision of the company that the press release is about. It's almost as great as a testimonial because it is written in the third person and sounds like news, not like you are bragging.

Once you write a press release, you should post it in a "latest news" section of your Web site. While this is a great first step, the next step is to syndicate the press release.

Syndicating press releases is similar to syndicating articles. At the end of every press release there is usually a section that explains who the company is and what they do. This is another great place to put a link to your Web site. When you syndicate the release, it will create inbound links to your site, which, as we discussed, are great for boosting your ranking in the search engines. Here is a sample of a format you can use:

About Dicks + Nanton Agency LLC: Dicks + Nanton Agency LLC celebrity brands entrepreneurs and professionals as experts in their field of business and helps them expand nationwide. JW Dicks, Esq. and Nick Nanton, Esq., attorneys by trade and entrepreneurs by choice, focus on helping their clients expand and make more money using specific proprietary systems including Exclusive Marketing Licenses™, Online Marketing Platforms™ and other creative business strategies. For more information about Dicks + Nanton Agency LLC visit www.DicksNantonAgency.com.

Here are a few great sites that you can use to syndicate your press releases:

1. www.prlog.org – free but very effective

2. www.prweb.com – this site has several levels of service to choose from and even offers podcasting and search engine optimization

3. www.prnewswire.com – similar to number two

For even more resources, visit the resources section of www.CelebrityBrandingYou.com.

Give it a shot. You'll be pleased to see how quickly your news will get picked up!

Phase III: Monitor, Optimize and Create New Revenue Streams

Marketing is a moving target. Just like building a Web site (Phase I) and not promoting the site (Phase II) is a bad idea, Phase III is equally important. The best part is, once you are aware of how the online world works, this is where you will discover a treasure chest of untapped markets. As you delve deeper into your online business to determine what works and what doesn't, you will find market niches that aren't being served. When you discover these markets, you can quickly reposition to serve that market with just a few tweaks of your current marketing, promotion and pay-per-click strategy.

This is ultimately what Phase III is, the opportunity to optimize your business and create new revenue streams.

What Works?

Some people suggest that they know in advance what will work. But while we all try to make the best educated guess we can, ultimately until you test something, everything is just that -- an educated guess. The market is ever changing and "what works" is a constantly moving target. This is the ongoing phase of your online business. It definitely takes some work, but without it you can quickly find yourself spending marketing money in the wrong places, and believe us, it goes quickly!

Monitoring and Reporting

As mentioned previously, you absolutely must monitor your online efforts in order to quickly shuffle your marketing efforts, and dollars, out of campaigns that aren't working and into campaigns that are generating income.

In order to monitor your traffic, there are many tools you can use; however, as usual, Google has given us some free tools, so we advocate using those!

Google Analytics: www.google.com/analytics.

This can be installed from your Google Ad Words account ,or, if you don't have one, go to the Web site above. All you have to do is enter your site information, and it will spit out a line of html code. Give this code to your web designer and Google Analytics will start tracking what happens on your Web site. It does more than we could possibly hope to explain to you in this book, but what we can tell you is that digging into the functionality of this software is very worthwhile, and extremely helpful in determining where traffic is coming from, and why the traffic is or is not hanging around long enough to convert into customers.

TIP: You may not want to install this code until after you have finished building your Web site. If you install it before you are done, all of the visits you, your designer and your friends give the site, can end up misleading you on how much traffic you are really getting.

Google Alerts: www.google.com/alerts

Did we mention that we love Google?! Google has given us all another free tool that allows us to stay up-to-date with where information about you is coming from and where it is posted.

What happens is that you can type any word into Google alerts, and then, when Google indexes a new Web page that contains the term(s) that you typed in, it alerts you.

Some great uses for Google Alerts are:

1. Tracking where your press releases are posted

2. Tracking where your articles are posted

3. Monitoring your competitors

4. Monitoring your industry

5. Keeping tabs on who is talking about you on their blog or Web site

There are an infinite number of other great uses as well; all you have to do is use your imagination!

We use both of these tools to monitor our own results and the results of our clients.

9

Promoting Yourself Offline

9

Promoting Yourself Offline

While we have all been wooed into the new millennium by the eCommerce possibilities thar are virtually cost-free worldwide communication strategies of the online landscape, we must not forget about traditional business principles and how to use the offline world to our advantage.

The boom of the Internet has truly been a blessing for many small businesses. However, in many instances, people have begun to rely too heavily on the Internet and forgotten the age old adage about what happens when you put all of your eggs in one basket. If anything happens to that basket, for any reason (whether it's your fault or not), you are in trouble. In this chapter, we are going to discuss seven of our favorite strategies for building a client base through your Celebrity Branding™ and increasing your cash flow in the offline world. Many of these strategies seem obvious, the beauty of them is exactly that -- they are obvious, but not many businesses take the time to execute them. And we can promise you one thing, if you implement these strategies, you will definitely stick out over and above the crowd of your competitors.

Seven Strategies for Increasing Profitability and Dominating Your Competition in the Offline World

1. Newsletters

This is "an oldie but a goodie." We're talking about real paper here people, the kind you have printed with ink that you can mail to your clients and prospects and hand out to everyone you meet.

A newsletter is really just a collection of information presented in any fashion you want. Some people choose to have them in color with bright photos on glossy paper, and others choose to print them on their laser printer in black and white with nothing but text. Both strategies work. The key factor to realize here is that this is a way to stay at the top of your clients' minds. *With a newsletter, they will receive whatever information you want to give them at whatever time intervals you choose to give it to them.*

You can fill your newsletter with the latest information in your industry that will make your clients take action and call you. For instance, if you are a mortgage broker and interest rates are at an all time low, wouldn't it be great to write a short article about how this can affect monthly payments and remind your clients that you can help them lower their payments because of the new rates? The possibilities are endless, and this works in every industry!

We have seen everyone from doctors, accountants, carpet cleaners, mortgage brokers, real estate agents, local restaurants and just about every business in between, use the newsletter strategy to drive business. Size doesn't matter. Your newsletter can be as long or as short as you'd like. You can include success stories from past clients, congratulations to clients who have used your product or service successfully to change their life, coupons for discounts on a featured product or service and much more.

A newsletter is essentially a way for you to speak to all of your clients and prospects every month, to let them know how you can help them, just like you've been helping others.

RESOURCE: Log onto the resources section of www.CelebrityBrandingYou.com for a source we set up to help you quickly and easily design, print and mail newsletters.

WARNING: Be prepared for people to get absolutely hooked on your newsletter. We have heard several stories about customers calling to ask why they hadn't received their newsletters yet because they always look forward to them in their mailboxes at a certain time of the month! Wouldn't you like to build a huge list of these loyal fans?

2. Card Campaigns

Everyone loves to receive a birthday card. It doesn't matter how old you are, it is nice to know someone is thinking of you. When was the last time you got a birthday card in the mail from someone who wasn't related to you? Yeah, that's the point. So, we set up a campaign that sends our clients birthday cards every year on their birthday. They are always very appreciative, and its just one more thing that we have done for them that no one else is doing consistently.

Another great strategy is to develop a campaign for sending out thank you notes to prospective clients after your first meeting as well as sending out thank you cards every time someone sends you a referral.

If you choose, you can do things the old-fashioned way with a spreadsheet of birthdays and hand write and hand address all of them. Using your own handwriting is clearly the most personal option, and when you have the time to do it, you should definitely do it this way. However, in the busy world in which most of us live, this isn't an easy way to do things.

We have a system that allows us to develop "campaigns" for sending out cards to our clients. We can set up birthday campaigns, thank you campaigns, referral campaigns or any other kind of campaign that we want. We then customize the message to include our client's name in the message. We can even have it printed to look like we hand wrote it. While this isn't quite as good as hand writing everything, it is certainly more efficient, and it's a real close second! If you're salivating at the thought of what you could do with a system like this, we won't keep you in suspense any longer. You can sign up and get started by visiting the resources section of www.CelebrityBrandingYou.com.

3. Public Relations

One of our favorite expressions is, "The world doesn't know what you're doing unless you take the time to tell them." Newsletters are a great strategy for telling your clients about what you're doing, but what about everyone else whose mailing addresses you don't have? That's where mass media comes in.

Through the use of press releases, you can tell the world what you're doing. By submitting press releases to your local news outlets including newspapers, magazines, periodicals, television stations and everyone else you can think of, you will get some press. The key is to make sure that what you are giving them is newsworthy. While it might be very exciting to you that you just upgraded the computers in your office, you are going to have to find a pretty enticing spin to get it picked up in the news. Also, be sure to adhere to standard press release format so your news doesn't end up in "the circular file" -- also known as the garbage can.

You can hire a public relations firm to handle this for you, you can hire a technical writer locally, you can hire off of a Web site like www.elance.com or you can use our recommended PR firm, www.NextLevelMediaOnline.com.

4. Radio Shows

Radio is still one of the most listened to forms of mass media. It's just so convenient when you are stuck in traffic or driving to and from just about anywhere. So, it makes sense to capitalize on it.

You can always buy air time to advertise on radio shows; however, a strategy that most people don't think of is to host your own radio show. You can buy blocks of airtime on local airwaves at cheaper rates than you'd probably think. You need to make sure that whatever airwaves you are buying are actually frequented by your target demographic, but similar to a newsletter, this medium allows you to dynamically interface with your prospective clients by talking to them for a specific period of time each week. (For the very brave, you can speak to them daily if you like!)

Think about it, when you hear someone on the radio, you automatically think they're an expert. After all, why would they be on the radio if they weren't an expert? If you use this strategy wisely, you can prospect on the air by having listeners call in with issues they'd like to discuss. Then you can impart your wisdom to them, just like you would normally do in a sales consultation, but you can do it so that the rest of the world can hear how great you are at what you do. It's another way you can leverage your time by consulting with thousands of people at the same time.

We know professionals who have done this, and there have been times when we have done this as well. It definitely makes the phone ring at your office! Not to mention, you can record the content on your show and re-purpose it as podcasts and audio clips on your Web site as well as CDs that you send to VIP clients, or a list of clients you know are interested in the topics discussed.

Being on the radio is a sure way to be seen as a Celebrity Expert by your surrounding community, and we encourage you to consider this often forgotten medium. If you don't want to appear on a show all the time, you can schedule guest appearances or even buy blocks of time where you play a prerecorded show. This works like an infomercial on radio and can do extremely well if you buy the right time slots.

5. Speaking at Seminars (or hosting your own).

If you live anywhere near a big city, you are likely missing out on many opportunities to speak to potential clients. In most major cities, there are trade shows and seminars held weekly. Not every one will have your ideal clients as attendees, but many of them will. Just think about this: if you got the opportunity to address 100-ideal clients at one time, don't you think you would get some new business? Well, what about speaking to more than 1,000-ideal clients? You could easily do this by speaking at one seminar or trade show a month. Don't you think you could do that?

Start paying attention to events held in your area as well as events held by trade associations of which you are a member. Often they are looking for interesting speakers who can bring a fresh topic to their conventions, because after all, that's what brings attendees and that's how they make their money. We have spoken with thousands of people who were featured speakers at seminars, as well as panelists at trade shows and events. The line of people who will rush you at the end of such an engagement is simply priceless.

If you don't live near a big city, and you don't have a lot of events coming through your area, you can always travel to the nearest city or to the nearest event that serves your target market. Or you can put on your own events. Remember, you don't have to have thousands or even hundreds of people in attendance; you just have to have the "right" people in attendance. Just think about how much value there is in speaking to multiple prospects in a setting where you are the featured lecturer or teacher.

Subconsciously, this takes your "students" back to grade school, and without even knowing it they hold you in high regard because you are the "teacher." In such a setting you are about to use role reversal to your benefit. Rather than visiting 20 or 30 decision makers in their offices and trying to convince them to do business with you, you are able to assemble the same group of decision makers in a setting that makes them realize you are the expert and lets them see how many people are considering doing business with you. Most smart business people don't let opportunities like this pass them up, and they will line up for "the opportunity" to work with such a highly esteemed and sought after expert!

Teleseminars are also a great tool. Although nothing is quite as good as speaking to your prospects in-the-flesh, your geographic reach is unlimited when you use teleseminars. Teleseminars are often formatted the same way as a traditional lecture. You can close off all of the lines if you want to be the only one speaking, and you can open them up when you'd like to take questions. You can set up free teleconferences by visiting www.freeconferencecall.com.

Whenever possible, you should video and audio record your presentations. Not only so that you can critique your presentations to make them better, but also so that you can re-purpose the content. You can often give these products you make to interested prospects, setting the stage for your Celebrity Expert status. The other alternative is to develop these materials into info products and sell them on your Web site or at seminars. To increase your income, turn this content into a course on your expert topic and sell it. Remember, as you begin selling info products, you are starting people on your ladder of ascension, getting them into your sales "pipeline" and working with the client to escalate them into top level clients.

6. Client-Continuity Campaign

This is another one of our favorite concepts. These campaigns are commonly known as "drip" campaigns. Similar to a dripping faucet, you continue to let your prospective clients know a little bit about your business each month, and you stay in front of them so that they begin to get to know you.

Here is a tentative outline for the first six months of a client-continuity campaign:

Month 1: Introductory Letter

This would introduce you and your services and invite prospects to contact you to learn more. It could possibly even invite them to attend a free event in their area or to log onto your Web site to receive a free special report or a free gift.

Month 2: Special Report

Mail out a printed copy of a special report that talks about a key topic of importance to your audience, it will educate them just enough to interest them in learning more from you. Don't be afraid to put a strong "call to action" in your report so clients know you are inviting them to contact you to learn more.

Month 3: Customized Postcard

This is a creative way to grab attention and give the prospect a specific reason to contact you. You should use this to promote a specific product, service or special offer. The benefit to a postcard is that your audience doesn't have to open it to read your message, and, nowadays, it is quick and inexpensive to personalize such postcards to really get you noticed. You can use full-color graphics, and you can even designate text on the postcard that can be changed on each card to incorporate your prospects' names. When created correctly, these create a great "buzz" and get a great response.

Month 4: Product/Service Brochure

This would be a deeper introduction to your products and services to explain them in detail. It should contain success stories from past clients as well as a special offer to try you out -- coupons work great for this.

TIP: On any printed materials, if you have blank space that isn't serving a purpose, consider inserting testimonials. It will build credibility and help you reinforce your strengths in space that would otherwise serve no purpose.

Month 5: Magazine Story/Personal Interest Article

This is a personal interest story that would look and feel as if it were taken right out of a magazine. It explains who you are, what you do and how you are different from others in your industry. You can take any angle you want with this, but one of our favorite angles is how you are "taking the world by storm and revolutionizing your industry." Rather than a boring biography, we like to do these because it really gives your potential client a way to learn about who you are in a unique way -- one that will motivate them to contact you. It will also further solidify your celebrity status in their mind.

Month 6: Audio CD Covering a Specific Topic

Use this as a tool similar to the magazine story. It is an opportunity for you to connect in another unique way with potential clients. They can drive around in their car and listen to you being interviewed or listen to you teaching, which will give them insight as to why you're the best. Not to mention you can use the time to subtly sell a particular product or service. It's a great tool, and not many people send out CDs for free, so you are much more likely to get noticed by them.

The possibilities are endless as to what you can send out to your clients. The more creative you are, the more likely you are to get noticed. Just remember to stick to a consistent message and give your clients only one opportunity at a time. If you give them too many opportunities to act within the same marketing piece, they are likely to get confused and not act at all. Also note, in this example of a six month campaign we have used several different media to deliver your message. Remember: change it up for interest and be creative.

7. Write a Book

We have mentioned this before, but it is worth repeating. Write a book. Imagine having your clients beg to spend eight, nine or more hours with you to listen to you tell them what your business philosophy is and how you can help them. This is exactly what you get to do with a book! The amount of time that you can get inside the head of your potential clients is endless, as long as your content is interesting. When this strategy is executed correctly, your clients should find your work insightful and will understand even more about what you do and how you are different than the rest of the industry.

This is another subconscious trigger that you need to be aware of. Most people never question the authority of a book. If someone writes a book, then the general public automatically grants them Celebrity Expert status. It's as simple as that.

Also, handing out your book is like handing out a 200-page business card. It will really impress potential clients. How many of your competitors have their own books?

Most people think it is difficult and expensive to publish a book or that you have to get a publishing deal, but this couldn't be further from the truth.

You can self-publish your book by having it printed by a printing company that specializes in books. You can find many such companies online by searching on your favorite search engine. One of our favorite options is www.booksurge.com. Book Surge is owned by Amazon.com and offers all of the services you need to publish your book. When you're done, they will even sell it on Amazon.com for you! You can also try www.lightningsource.com for a competitive pricing quote. They will even print the contents of your book in color.

Content for your Book

You can certainly write all of your own content for your book, but if you don't like writing or simply don't have the time, you can hire someone to write it for you. These individuals are called ghostwriters and you can find them locally or by searching for them online. You can even find them on Web sites like www.elance.com.

Another great strategy for creating content is to follow the formula that created multi-million dollar success for entrepreneurs Jack Canfield and Mark Victor Hansen with their "Chicken Soup for the Soul" series. This strategy is pure genius. These guys had people from all around the world submit their own stories. Then they compiled them, printed them and sold them. You can do the same thing! Have each of your clients write a case study about working with you, or solicit gurus in each field that you want to discuss and ask them if they would like to submit a chapter to be published in your book. By having multiple people take on the burden of writing chapters of the book, you greatly lessen the burden on yourself.

These are just a few of the strategies that we use in the offline world, your imagination will help you find many, many more.

The key to remember when using offline strategies is that many of your competitors have simply gotten too cheap and too lazy to creatively market. If you implement even one or two of these strategies, you will set yourself apart from your competitors and further solidify your Celebrity Expert status in the minds of your target market.

STAGE 4

Rollout: Expanding Your Celebrity Brand Business

10

Capitalize And Rollout Your Celebrity Brand

10

Capitalize And Rollout Your Celebrity Brand

Congratulations! You should now see the how the process of "Celebrity Branding You™" works and understand the potential it holds for you to expand your business and eliminate your competition. We now want to expose you to the "next level" of Celebrity Branding™. We will show you how to capitalize on what you have accomplished to deliver the kind of money you always wanted to make.

At this point of the Celebrity Branding™ process, you have built a good name for yourself on a local level. You have created methods to bring in prospects and convert them to customers. You have written a book or at least special reports displaying your expertise. You may have started speaking to local groups or created your own seminar program. Whatever you have done, you have created a process. Once you have a process that is successful, you have created great value in the form of intellectual property that can be sold over and over again. This intellectual property in the form of a business system can be packaged and duplicated all over the country by different people who are in the same business, service or profession as you. You can do this by creating a marketing package for your system and selling that package along with training or coaching to others in your line of business or even other businesses for a substantial fee.

If the concept of creating a system for your business and a national expansion of it doesn't immediately click for you, think in terms of a franchise. By their very nature, successful franchises are centered on a proven system of operation and then expanded throughout the country to individuals who believe in the system and want to execute it in their local market. Your proven system of operation combined with an offer of an area-exclusive license to a person in every city across America, who pays you a fee to use your system, is similar in operation. While not all experts who do these national rollouts add the area-exclusive element, doing so tends to increase the value of what you have to offer.

While this next level of business growth can be intimidating, the millions of dollars that you can generate from it will make it all worthwhile. Yes, we said millions of dollars. While we don't want you to think of this as a get-rich-quick program, we do want to encourage you to believe in the possibilities and think of it as a wealth-building system for you and your family because there are many people doing this in all types of industries.

Let us give you some examples.

Craig Proctor:

Craig is a real estate coach who does marketing for Realtors all over the country. You can review his Web site at www.quantumleapsystem.com.

Craig is interesting as a real estate coach because he is also an active Realtor, practicing what he preaches. He perfected his marketing system on a local level and has now taken it across the country and offers other Realtors the opportunity to take what he does successfully and copy it in their market. Like a franchise, the concept is that a well-done system with a proven record of accomplishment will work the same in one town as it does in another. When you go to his Web site, pay close attention to the coaching section to get an idea of how this works for him. Craig has a very specific program that lasts for 12 months. This is just one way coaching programs work, and we will show you other models.

Dan Kennedy:

Dan Kennedy is one of the premiere marketing coaches in the country. He has a library of products and services to get you involved with him and his organization, and once you do -- it is very difficult to leave. The reason it is so hard to leave is because what he teaches and what he sells rings true. Once you find someone who is good at what they do, when you need what they have to offer, you become very loyal. You can visit Dan's site at www.DanKennedy.com.

As you look at Dan's products and services, note how carefully he relies on giving you irresistible offers backed by long guarantees. He does everything he can to get you involved, but if what you buy is not right for you, he makes it easy for you to leave and get your money back. The reason for this approach is that he does not want to hassle with people or waste time. A quick sale is not the point. He is trying to build a valuable, lifetime customer. Of course, this is an important lesson in itself.

As you look at Dan Kennedy's Web sites, note that he uses numerous levels of customer participation and client ascension to take you through the processes -- just as we have discussed in this book.

Jerry Jones:

Jerry Jones is The Personal Dental Coach. He has positioned himself as one of the top marketing specialists in the dental industry. Jerry combines his national program with multiple ways to stay in touch with him including both personally and in groups. For instance, his $297 per month program includes a weekly fax; 12 coaching calls, where you can speak one-on-one with Jerry for 15 minutes; eight group tele-conferences; four monthly audio seminars; two personal meetings in a group and various other benefits that bring value to the presentation. His Web sites are www.JerryJonesDirect.com and www.EMCdental.com.

In addition to his dental coaching, Jerry has also carved out a niche in the crowded real estate field with a real estate boot camp targeted to dentists: www.RealEstateForBusyDentists.com.

Bill Glazer:

Bill is a business partner of Dan Kennedy. His marketing background was centered around owning and operating a super successful up-scale menswear store. Through his personal success, he expanded his knowledge to other menswear stores in the country serving as their coach and teaching them how to better market their stores. He now has an advanced coaching group for all businesses. The advanced groups are called Peak Performers, and, at the time of this writing, they pay him $779 per month. This fee includes the Gold+ program of Bill and Dan's that alone sells for $297 per month. The additional money gives you three, two-day group meetings in person with Bill and his co-host Lee Milteer. The group meeting offers the advantage of personal contact and the dynamics of networking with other like-minded people who clearly prove they are serious about business because they are paying a fee to be a part of the group. The fee alone is a good qualifier. You can visit his Web site at www.bgsmarketing.com.

Robert Skrob:

Robert is a consultant/coach who teaches people how to set up their own associations. An association can be either a stand-alone profit center for a specialty niche market, or it can be an additional source of revenue for coaches and/or companies that want to use the association structure to provide various additional benefits to members. Robert teaches a two-day, $5,000 class about how to set up your own association, or he will run the association for you on a consulting fee basis. He has set up associations for many industries including real estate, mortgage brokerages, retail supply, cosmetic surgery, restaurants, the info-marketing business and more. In fact, there is not an industry that could not gain from this program. Robert's Web site is www.AssociationsforInfoMarketers.com.

Chris Hurn:

Chris is a commercial lender who specializes in a somewhat obscure SBA loan (the SBA 504) that allows business people to buy their own building instead of leasing. He has taken his knowledge of this program along with his marketing skills and created a system for getting clients for other commercial lenders throughout the country who do not have the marketing savvy that Chris does. He charges these "correspondents" a sizeable fee to participate in this program, and then he participates in their deal flow. In turn, the local brokers increase their profits because of Chris's skill. Visit his Web site at www.504experts.com.

These are but a few specific examples of successful entrepreneurs who have taken their local success, Celebrity Branded themselves and gone national. The businesses are varied and include: restaurant operators, carpet cleaners, foreclosure experts and dental schools. The financial results are extremely lucrative for those who succeed and take their business to this "next level."

In our examples, we have tried to deliver a factual look at these businesses and what they offer without adding any sort of hype. If you search for them online, you will see that they are not quite so bashful. We do not want you to think that we feel there is anything wrong with tooting your own horn either. In fact, we think that is what "Celebrity Branding You™" is all about -- promoting yourself, delivering an irresistible offer and backing it up by unqualified guarantees. That is why the people we have described here are so successful.

For a detailed list of other national rollout programs, visit our rollout resourse section at www.CelebrityBrandingYou.com.

The Exclusive Marketing License™

There are several ways to structure your system for national rollout. A moment ago we alluded to the well-known franchise concept. The big advantage of the franchise concept is that it is a "well-known" concept that many people are already familiar with. When you talk to people about owning a franchise, they have heard of that type of business-operating system, so you do not have to explain the concept.

Instead, you can focus your time and energy on selling the franchise itself.

The difficulty with franchise systems is that they are expensive to launch and many people don't want to risk a significant amount of money on something they believe will work but may not have the full confidence to back their belief with dollars. Others simply don't have the money.

The Exclusive Marketing License™ (EML) is a solution to the financial dilemma. An EML is structured to have many of the benefits of the franchise without all of the regulatory costs normally associated with it. We have spent a great deal of time and money in our law firm carefully structuring the EML to be exempt from franchise rules and business opportunity laws. Additionally, we monitor the laws for changes and adapt the EML agreements to them. For example, there is legislation proposed for a new federal business opportunity disclosure law, which will likely require some sort of disclosures for anyone who sells even a basic coaching service. This will not present a problem for our clients because they will simply follow the rules. Frankly, we always suggest full-disclosure to your clients of every aspect of your program because you are building a long-term relationship with them, not simply trying to make a one-time sale.

How the EML Works

Despite our own spin, the Exclusive Marketing License™ isn't a new concept. In fact, large companies and big celebrities such as the NFL, NBA, Disney, Universal Studios, Tiger Woods, Dan Marino and every college in America all use some variation of a license agreement to let others use their name for a fee. Some of the companies and celebrities combine the standard product license with an exclusive territory to create an entity structure similar to our EML. You are now going to experience similar success by licensing your own proven business process. Let's walk you through an example.

Assume for a moment that you are in the real estate business. You have created a specialty for yourself working with investors. You have chosen this specialty because unlike the residential sales market, you aren't affected when retail sales are down. Investors are always buying real estate, in good times or bad, because there are different reasons to purchase real estate in different economies. For example, if the market is overbuilt and sales are down, this is precisely the time to look for bargains in foreclosures. If the market is strong, they may be looking for real estate that has development potential or strong cash flow. The point is -- there is always a market for the investor.

If you were this real estate person, you could follow our process for Celebrity Branding™.

Stage #1: Finding your Niche

In our example, you already know your niche. You are a real estate investment expert in the community you serve.

Stage # 2: Creating your Brand

First, you would define yourself as the expert in the real estate investment field. In doing so, you would create your "ladder of ascension" (see chapter 7) for people to learn about you. Normally, you would start off the program with a free product or seminar. One way this has been successfully accomplished is to sponsor local lunches where the investors could come to hear you or a guest talk about the real estate market. The first lunch would be free, and then you could charge the investors a monthly fee to continue attending. Typically, the first level of your ladder of client ascension is low cost or free because you want as many prospects as possible to get to know you and identify you as the expert in this field. So, to increase attendance, you hold the cost down for the investor. Don't rush to make a sale. Building relationships in a rush is not the best way to build for the long term.

After investors have participated in the lunches, they are offered an opportunity to move up your ladder of ascension and get in on the inside track for investments in your area. Usually this is a paid service and pricing varies, starting at about $39.95 per month or higher, depending on the level of work or educational process you are providing.

Following through effectively with the first level of service you offer leads to offerings of higher levels of coaching or an opportunity for the client to hire you as his exclusive "buyer's broker." Such an agreement promises that if they buy any real estate, they will buy from you and no one else, in exchange for the work and education you are providing. This buyer's broker arrangement eliminates the need for prospecting because you have a built-in investor list that is always looking for the properties you find.

In some cases, programs like the one we just went through offer an even higher service and, of course, higher fees ($250 to $500 per month) for investors who want to get the "first look" at any of the properties you find. Naturally, you will see that you are getting paid some impressive numbers from these investors just to be a part of your valued "inner circle." This fee can be added on top of your commissions or credited against any commission you earn. Either way, you have a monthly income stream even if you do not sell anything.

Stage #3: Developing Your Celebrity Expert Status

In this stage you begin to add to your Celebrity Expert status. You build your online presence in the form of your online marketing platform. Offline, you attend charity functions to increase your profile, write articles and do press releases. In our real estate example, a book written by you or a ghostwriter would help to boost your credibility.

Stage #4: Rollout – Nationally Expanding Your Celebrity Brand Business

Package your Exclusive Marketing License™ real estate program and sell it to other real estate professionals. You will grant them a marketing license for all of the processes you have proven to build your business locally.

This brings our example to where we are in this chapter. You have built your online and offline, marketing- and business-development system. You know which direct mail pieces work best to get people to your events. You know what type of speakers you should have as guests. You have designed a buyer's broker contract that works and has real legal teeth. All of these concepts are a part of your system to work with real estate investors. Now, you package this system and offer it to Realtors outside your area in other cities who would like to work with investors but do not know how. You system is the answer.

Question: How much would you pay to someone who had

a proven system like the one we described if you were in the real estate business? Before you answer, think about it. Yes, you would spend some money, but you would get marketing that was already proven to work. All you would have to do is follow the system. Sounds good doesn't it?

The answer to how much someone will pay at this time seems to be somewhere between $15,000 and $40,000 per area exclusive territory. How many areas of exclusive territories do you have to offer? Just for fun, let's say 400. Additionally, we will assume the up-front fee you charge for your program to be $20,000. What's the sell out value to you? $8,000,000.

While $8,000,000 is nothing to sneeze at, here is where the real interest will kick in for you. All of these programs also have a residual or "continuity" fee that goes with them. There are some very high ones, but typically they range from $487 per month to $1,000 per month. The residual fee is for continued support, coaching and ongoing new marketing ideas that you will provide your Exclusive Marketing Licensees™.

Now for the math. Assume you are able to sell 400 areas times the low range of fees, $487. This gives you a monthly residual income of $194,800 per month. Annually, this works out to $2, 337,600. Exciting, don't you think?

What if you can't sell 400 territories? Well you can, but let's assume you can only sell 100. In the case of the 100 at $487 per month, it still provides you with a residual income each month of $48,870. In addition, do not forget you still have your original local group you started with. Impressive, don't you agree?

We think the EML is truly one of the most exciting ways to

build a successful business in the country today. Remember, our example was for real estate, but all industries can do this: doctors, lawyers, mortgage brokers, carpet cleaners, financial planners, online business gurus, health trainers, you name it. *If a person has a successful business, they can brand themselves as a celebrity and charge a healthy sum to teach others to do the same.*

And you know what? There is more…in the final stage for you to learn!

STAGE 5
Selling Your Business and Creating "Legacy Dollars"

11

Formulate An Exit Plan

11

Formulate An Exit Plan

We hope you have become energized with excitement and that your brain is bursting with great ideas for your business and what you can do with it. While you may build and enjoy this business for many years, at some point you will want to consider selling it in order to monetize the value of what you have created. Your desire to sell might be in order to retire and enjoy life, or it may be to free up your time, take some money off the table and build another business to rollout again.

No matter what you desire, here are some options you have created for yourself:

1. Sell the income stream produced from your royalty or continuity payments to a buyer/investor or one of your licensees.

2. Combine the EMLs in a city or state and sell off that part of your business to an investor or one of your licensees to take over.

3. Roll up all the licensees into one large company and sell to an institutional buyer. (This gives the licensees an opportunity to monetize their value as well.)

4. Roll up all of the licensees as suggested in #4, but also add their companies to the sale creating a larger sale.

5. Roll up all of the licensees and their companies into a single company, and take the company public through an IPO.

While a detailed discussion of each of these exit strategies is beyond the scope of this book, they are exciting to see as real possibilities. While this final exit plan has been done many times for franchise systems, we have not seen it done yet for the Exclusive Marketing License program, but we hope to be able to report one soon. In fact, we hope to be able to report that it is YOURS!

12

The Final Chapter – What's Next?

12

The Final Chapter – What's Next?

As of the time of writing this book, the strategies we have outlined are cutting edge, but we all know that things change and we must all find "the next big thing."

Just as those of you who are successful in life and in business know that you can't expect to stay at the top of your industry if you relax once you reach the pinnacle of success, we also know that you will need to stay on top of your Celebrity Branding™ process. In order to make this easy for you we've created www.CelebrityBrandingYou.com for you to keep up with all of the newest tips and strategies that we uncover as we continue to work with some of the biggest and best in the business.

Be sure to visit www.CelebrityBrandingYou.com to sign-up for our free CelebrityZine™ as well as to find many great resources that you can use so you won't be left behind. We look forward to hearing about your success and welcome your correspondence.

We can be reached at:

JW Dicks, Esq.
JWDicks@DicksNanton.com
800-981-1403

Nick Nanton, Esq.
NDNanton@DicksNanton.com
800-981-1403

Here's to the bringing out the Celebrity in You!

Jack & Nick

BONUS SECTION

Special Reports for Growing Your Income Today

13

Top 10 Ways to Grow Your Business Fast

13

Top 10 Ways To Grow Your Business Fast

Unlike some of the David Letterman top 10 lists, which give you a list of items in reverse order of their importance, each one of the 10 ways to grow your business fast is important. The most import is the one you think your business can implement quickly and efficiently. That strategy will differ depending on where you are in the growth cycle, and what you may have already implemented in the past.

As you read the list, you will see some strategies that you might be familiar with but haven't implemented because you didn't think it applied to your business. Try not to just skip over the strategy, but consider it a moment in your present circumstance, which may have changed such that revisiting the idea may now be fruitful.

Another interesting way to view the list is not just with an eye on your own business, but on the business of others you may come in contact with. Few people have ever stopped to think about working on other people's businesses like we do every day. However, we suggest that you might consider this growth opportunity for yourself. Some of you have become successful at executing one or several of these strategies. So successful, that the knowledge becomes a growth strategy for you in and of itself. The reason is because you now have the ability to help others "see" the opportunity and collect a fee for advising them, or take it a step further and help them implement the growth strategy in their business. You work on the business strategy with them in a joint-venture capacity.

Good ideas for business growth are a dime a dozen. Having the knowledge and ability to implement them is the key element to success. With that said, lets take a look at the strategies.

1. Joint Ventures (JV) and Strategic Alliances (SA)

While joint ventures are nothing new to the business world, its use is accelerated through the web and e-commerce. Offers of creating strategic alliances (SA) are commonplace in the wired world in particular, and many of these quick relationships develop over time into the more formal arrangement of a JV.

From a terminology standpoint, SAs are less formal and a precursor to a formal JV. While SAs are created on the fly (quickly formed and often quickly dissolved) JVs take more time, structure and documentation. This is not required legally, but it is the way people think of their structure.

Both the SA and JV are formed for many reasons, but here are some examples:

- Joint promotion of products or creation of a special event

- Developing a new product or service
- Developing a new market such as an international expansion
- Developing or sharing new technology
- Creating common distribution channels
- Pooling resources of capital, intellectual property, employees or physical property

All of these types of inter-company relationships have been formed as either SAs or JVs, and all have been both successes and failures. The problem, of course, is not the structure, but the people or entities behind the structure that make or break the deal. Some people aren't cut out to deal well with others in a business relationship any more than some people don't seem to do well in marriages. Both require a lot of effort on the part of both parties, and some people are unable to get beyond their own objectives to see that the relationship works for both parties. Because of the potential problems that can come up in either of these business structures, a simple rule develops. The more money that is at stake, the more care and attention should be placed on formally structuring a legal relationship that does not risk either party's current business.

2. Licensing

Licensing has become big business today and is a great money generator because in most cases it is an extension of what your business does, as opposed to being the product or service that drives the train. There are exceptions to this generalization, of course, and there are even large companies that focus only on buying products or businesses that can be licensed.

The reason that licenses are so profitable is that the cost

of developing the licensed goods or services has already been spent, and the license agreement is now sold on the basis of a percent of gross sales. This means that the licensor has no responsibility for ongoing overhead or other worries affecting the traditional bottom-line aspects of the business.

The law around licensing is that you transfer to another party certain "rights" to the product or service as opposed to ownership. These rights can be broad use, or they can be structured with limited use and restrictions. The structure of the license requires great balance. The more restrictive you are in granting the license, the more control you have and the greater value of your remaining license rights as the licensor. On the other hand, if you are too restrictive so that the licensee cannot make money, you as the licensor won't either, and your opportunity to sell more will decline.

When people think of licensing, they often think of character licensing such as Winnie the Pooh, Mickey Mouse and Spiderman. Additionally, sports organizations such as the NFL, NBA and NASCAR have extremely successful licensing divisions. On the other side of the business spectrum, there is considerable licensing in software, biotechnology and telecom. These are all examples of big-business licensing producing millions of dollars for the licensor and huge opportunities for the licensee.

While big businesses profit from licensing, so can small businesses, and you should keep your eye out for opportunities. Strong databases are frequently opportunities available for licensing or "renting" for businesses that have done a good job of documenting their customers and collecting email and home addresses. These lists of buyers are very valuable to other businesses that might have a complementary product. Offering license rights to the other businesses gives them the opportunity to have additional prospects that would otherwise cost them more money than they are spending for your license. The license you agree to may be a one-time use, or it may be continuous. Additionally, the license may develop into a larger strategic alliance or JV if the license is a success.

Licensing can also play an important role in the growth of young companies, and used this way it can be a form of expansion capital. For example, your young company may not have the cash to expand into the international market with a product that has been successful in the U.S. Instead of waiting to have the expansion capital and losing time, you could license the right to your product overseas to one or more licensees who promise to put up money and promote the product in the new marketplaces. Yes, you may give up some of the potential profits that you might have made if you pulled it off by yourself, but the current license fees and the first mover advantage you get by acting now could far outweigh the "potential" you might lose.

3. Growth Through E- Commerce

The web has been with us long enough now that everyone should have a web presence, but not all do. Equally bad, many companies have Web sites that are outdated or that are little more than a business card on a computer.

Web sites and the strategy of effective e-commerce are a necessity for a company looking to grow. Your e-commerce plan must be one of capturing potential customers and moving them into the buying process instead of standing around waiting for someone to find you and hope they stumble on your contact information. Buzzwords such as search engine optimization (SEO), while passé to technophiles, are important strategic business tactics for companies in the growth mode. Why wait for a customer to find you when you can go find a customer? This is the essence of having a real e-commerce strategy for your business, and quite frankly this is the same strategy that separates successful businesses in the offline world.

Ask yourself an important question, "What is your e-commerce strategy?" Does it have its own plan of business operation, or is it just a supplement to your current business plan without any regard for its own budget and financial plans. Why miss the additional revenue offered through the online world? And do not wait for the "right time" to get started. The right time may never come, and you cannot recover the business you actually lose every day; time is very valuable.

While we think you should take advantage of each opportunity and strategy you have available, you may not always have the time or resources. This is when you begin to combine some of these strategies we are going through. In this case, if you cannot afford to, or do not know how to take advantage of e-commerce, consider spinning that part of your business into an entirely different company with its own budget. You might even consider this part of your business for funding by an investor. Leave the e-commerce application to someone who is a specialist in the online world, and let them create enhanced opportunities that you are missing today. The new mantra of today is to open your business and let others create advantages that you don't have the resources to pull off.

Another opportunity to consider, if you are short on time or money for an e-commerce presence, is to consider licensing your e-commerce intellectual property to someone who is an expert at e-commerce. Since you may never reach your potential for your own e-commerce strategy on your own, joint venture it with someone for a percentage of the business.

4. Ideas and Concepts

Generally speaking, an idea or a concept does not qualify for a patent, copyright, trade secret or trademark protection. You will lose the potential economic benefit of the idea or concept if you voluntarily disclose it unless you can satisfy three rules:

1. The idea is in a concrete form
2. The idea is original and useful
3. The idea is disclosed in a situation where a business relationship is planned and compensation paid

While meeting this test is not always easy to prove, the use of a non-disclosure agreement (NDA) and a non-circumvention agreement will help you prove elements of the test have been met. On the other hand, these agreements can also be an impediment to getting an opportunity to make a presentation. Many large companies are taking the flat position that they will not sign an NDA because would-be inventors are using contracts so broad that other potential opportunities could later be brought into the web of inclusion.

If you have a good idea, you should definitely try to profit from it. Creating specialized NDAs that are very specific may get you past the gate keepers, or sometimes you may just decide to take the risk and let the deal out and then memorialize the discussion you had with the other party, in writing, to demonstrate proof of your disclosure. Neither is a perfect approach, but it is the cost of doing business; sometimes you will not get compensated when you think you should.

Concepts that you already use in your business are a little easier to protect. This may be everything from a new way of marketing a product to developing a procedure of distribution that has not been used before. One way to capitalize on this information is through the consulting format. This strategy can be very lucrative over the years for the consultant who truly has information that can help someone save a great deal of time and money when implemented. Why wouldn't you use them?

Some other examples of ideas or concepts through non-tangible assets would be:

- Inventing and exploiting new products or services
- Opening new distribution channels
- New production and training techniques
- New promotional marketing campaigns
- Establishing new price methods or pricing structures

5. Real Estate Opportunities

Few companies view real estate as a corporate growth vehicle until it hits them in the head. McDonald's is a classic example. After opening thousands of stores in prime locations all across the country, it discovered it had amassed and held billions of dollars worth of real estate. It is not alone either. Other franchises learned from the McDonald's discovery, and are capitalizing by selling off their real estate assets to public REITs, some of which they had a hand in forming. These franchises not only make money on the initial sale, profiting over their basis in the real estate, but they also collect ongoing property management fees and sometimes a percentage of growth of the asset. By looking at a traditional business expense differently, they turned it into an asset with huge economic added value.

Smaller companies have also experienced growth through real estate by using their office needs as a way to buy real estate. Owner-occupied property is always easier to get good financing on, and after a company owns the real estate for a few years and sees appreciation, it can sell the property. It is easier to sell commercial property with a lease attached if a company agrees to be a tenant for a few years. A few years later, repeat the process and buy a new property to occupy.

Strategic use of your own company's needs can also leverage you into bigger properties. For example, in our current economy, most banks require pre-leasing on new construction. A company can develop a piece of property that is bigger than its own needs and make money on the sale of the additional property. An alternative, if you aren't an experienced developer, would be to joint venture the property with a developer who gets a fee for his work, but you make the spread between construction cost and the new value after development.

6. Mergers and Acquisitions (M&A)

M&A is always an exciting item of business news, as billions of dollars change hands with each merger or acquisition. However, these are usually just the headliners. Smaller, but perhaps just as important, transactions occur where local businesses buy competitors or complementary businesses. For example, a printer can either grow by increasing his marketing efforts, or he can grow by acquiring other print shops. By acquiring other shops, the buyer can make money immediately on the acquisition spread or by synergistic savings when the companies merge. The saving on these mergers or acquisitions come from many possibilities, including staff reduction, price increases because competition is eliminated, and leveraged intangible assets such as cross selling to a new database that one company had but the other didn't.

Mergers and acquisitions require some specialized knowledge to make sure you are not being taken advantage of, but generally these potential problems are learned and ironed out during your first acquisition experience. Future acquisitions become more formulaic, based on how the first was structured and modified as adjustments are needed.

Growth through mergers and acquisitions can also have a second advantage. Not only can you profit from the immediate synergy, but also as a company becomes larger it becomes a more interesting acquisition prospect to even larger companies that are willing to pay higher multiples. This means a possible increase in profit potential just on the arbitrage factor of smaller company value vs. larger.

7. Franchise

Other than e-commerce, franchise growth opportunities may be one of the biggest for you and your company. There are several layers of potential. Layer 1 is the opportunity to create your own franchise that grows into a huge number of stores. Layer 2 is the opportunity to buy into someone else's franchise in the early stage and get a master franchise for a strong territory. This could come about by spotting a successful West Coast franchise just starting to spread its wings and locking in the right to the South, or even a just a big state like Florida. Starbucks franchises made fortunes for people who early on found the little coffee shop in Seattle and decided to latch on.

Another less-traditional opportunity comes in adding a successful franchise to your existing non-competing but complementary business. For example, a printing company might add a sign franchise and put it into its existing storefront. The two companies would get a cost savings on doubling up on space and employees, while cross selling to each others' customers with different needs. This business move would add a whole new line of products with less incremental cost attached. The local print shop might benefit from the national name and exposure, and the franchise could benefit from the local reputation of the print business.

8. Intellectual Property (IP)

Intellectual property of all types is a way of growing a business. Patents, trademarks and copyrights on products or materials can be licensed, franchised, spun off or sold to produce additional revenues for a business.

Even names themselves have become highly marketable. Key domain names sell for multi millions, but even smaller names can be sold for five- and six-figure incomes. We have sold this type of intellectual property for clients and even ourselves. Once you train yourself to see the opportunity, bundle the domain name in a package that includes a functioning web site or a trademark. Do that extra IP work and you have an even more valuable commodity to sell.

We encourage our clients to regularly take an intellectual property audit of what they have that they could sell to someone who might be interested in building a business around it.

Simply trademarking great names that you own or use can be a terrific part-time job opportunity.

9. International Expansion

Clearly, the world is getting smaller, and ventures are taking place all over between people who never dreamed they would be doing business together because of previous geographical constraints. Now, all businesses have an opportunity to expand internationally either through e-commerce or by using the web as a way of finding contacts and sources that can help overseas. It is a lot easier to find people and contacts through the web as opposed to having to go overseas and start blindly, seeking distributions channels for your product.

Additionally, other countries want to take advantage of American products and know-how. Entrepreneurs in these countries seek out Americans with products and services to introduce to their country and marketplace. People may not like America's politics, but they like Americans, and they like the opportunities they can have working with an American business.

If you have products or services you think would do well internationally, join some of the respected international chambers of commerce that can help you get connected in a country for a small investment in their membership. The reverse is equally true if you want to import products from across the ocean. Seek out information about who to do business with from a specific country's trade organization or chamber of commerce.

10. Consulting and Training

In the past, consultants have had a stigma of not being able to do anything on their own so they went into the field of consulting or teaching. While this can still be true, consulting has turned into big business again as everyone from Bill Clinton to Donald Trump is willing to lend their name, expertise or connections in exchange for a fee.

Consulting or deal making is a new form of intellectual property power that takes the form of mentoring or lobbying on behalf of people or companies who do not have the contacts or experience in a certain area of specialty. Additionally, consulting and training are huge time savers. It is often said it is not the things you know that kill you in a business endeavor, it is the things you do not know. Using someone with experience who can guide you along the growth path at a faster and safer clip can be worth its weight in gold. This fact is particularly true in this fast-paced world, where someone else might be creating the same idea you are, right now, and it is a race to the market with the first one there winning all the chips. Do not short change yourself. Learn to spend money to make money, particularly if it can be at a faster pace with a leveraged return of multiple times the return on your investment.

If you are successful or have a unique knowledge base, consider offering it to others who you could help slash the learning curve and help them save money or make more. As long as you can show the potential client a good return on investment that he will make with you, he should be quick to take up the opportunity.

In summary, each of the 10 strategies mentioned can be a powerful addition to your business growth. Most companies never get beyond the implementation of a few, so by the addition of even one more to your arsenal, it can make a dramatic impact on the bottom line.

14

8 Power Principles to Make More Money While Working Less

14

8 Power Principles To Make More Money While Working Less

The idea of working less while making more is a daydream that society has been enjoying for decades, but as time goes by we seem to be doing just the opposite. The idea of taking control of our lives sounds like a "pie-in-the-sky" scheme, but Nick Nanton, a partner with the Dicks + Nanton Agency, said if you follow his structure of how life should be, your productivity and bank account will increase and your stress level will decrease. He has developed eight power principles to help you generate more money and free time while working less in today's 21st-century work environment.

The Dicks + Nanton Agency is a multimedia and marketing firm that specializes in Celebrity Branding™ clients. Nanton said they turn their clients into "celebrities" in their business so that their clients have a greater opportunity to lock out their competition and increase their profits. He said any businessperson can take advantage of this kind of marketing; whether a rug cleaner or a handyman; a doctor or corporate CEO.

The 1st Power Principle - Developing "The System"

If any business is going to be efficiently operated, proper management of time and money is imperative. Methods of doing less and earning more are concepts we've all thought about, but most of us probably haven't given it much credence. Frankly, from childhood we are groomed to work hard. It is in our nature to get up in the morning and prepare for a hard day's work. But, if we're honest with ourselves, sometimes we get off track and become too focused on the job and little else. We all need to stop and enjoy life now and then, and Nanton said people in business today need to learn to develop systems that will help save time and effort.

"When you create systems for your work, you'll find that you can grow your business exponentially. When we start a small business, we normally have to do everything ourselves. What we need to learn to do is take our "secret sauce" that we've developed and turn it into a system so that anyone can follow the formula, either as a whole plan or in pieces."

"Many entrepreneurs just don't feel comfortable sharing their personal workload -- that is the problem. They either feel guilty or they are too frugal, and they continue to try to do everything themselves. For an example, I'm a lawyer, so I'll give a legal example because lawyers are actually pretty good at this, but only because it has become customary. We create a system for what we do well, or more likely what can only be done by a lawyer, and then we can turn over the non-legal portions of the business -- the research segments -- to someone else. The lawyer can then review the findings, analyze the results, make the decisions and then spit out a legal action plan for what needs to happen or draft the necessary contract. With a system like this, you can use your "highest and best use of time" by creating a system that allows someone to step in and help you complete your workload so you can do more of the work you get paid more for and less of the work that either doesn't have enough value, you aren't very good at or you simply don't like doing."

But another habit that can be dangerous to an entrepreneur is the mentality of, "I'm the only one who can do this particular task the right way." They want to get their hands dirty, and sometimes these unique business people are very possessive about their business. Nanton said this is quite often the biggest hurdle to the issue of creating systems and outsourcing projects to other people. "You have to focus on doing the things that you do well, but you need to create a step-by-step guide of how you do things in your business. Take the time to consider the various tasks that keep your business running and write out a step-by-step system so anyone could walk in and accomplish the end goal with little direction. Having a system will help you in the event that someone has a life- altering incident that prevents them from coming to work for six months. By having a system, you guarantee the job will continue to be accomplished no matter who shows up for work on any particular day. It will really take a lot of the burden off of the business owner. Then, all you have to do is monitor the system while accomplishing the tasks that are more relevant and, more importantly, make you the most money.

The 2nd Power Principle - The Importance of Scalability

If you can create a scalable system to assist you in running your business, you will be able to exponentially grow your profits as well. Nanton explained, "Scalability is the concept of doing the same amount of work while reaping greater reward. Most people are excited when they hear that. Let's use the example of a business coach. If I'm a business coach, I can teach you over the phone, one on one, or I could set up a teleconference where I could teach 1,000 people the same concept at the same time. So, I would be doing the same amount of work in the form of teaching a concept, but instead of sharing the information with just one person, a teleconference could expand my reach without taking any more of my time. Essentially, the main concept of scalability is that it is possible to sell 1,000 people into the conference, and while it may cost you a few extra cents per person, you're doing the same amount of work while getting paid by 1,000 people versus just one. That's powerful."

The 3rd Power Principle – Outsourcing

This principle is a concept that many of today's Fortune 500 companies have already embraced, but it is still one that most small businesses may not have even considered. We see in the news almost every week, that companies are shedding personnel in order to get "lean and mean" and more profitable.

The old way of doing business is to hire a bunch of people, bring them into the office and make them sit at their desks and do their jobs (or more likely surf the Internet all day and not do their jobs). Think about what you are doing, as the business owner, when you create this obsolete business structure. You wake up at the same time each morning, eat the same breakfast and travel the same route to work; you've just created your own rat race. Rather than using this method of doing business, we advocate taking advantage of technology. We have access to every communication medium imaginable: teleconferencing, video conferencing; email, instant messaging, online message boards, cell phones and wireless email devices like BlackBerries and iPhones.

Using today's technology, you don't need to be surrounded, in person, by a bunch of capital-intensive employees. You can have 99 percent of the tasks performed by an outsourced person off site that you could have performed by someone who sits in your office, draining your resources each and every day whether you have something productive for them to do or not. In today's market, you can outsource anywhere at anytime, whether it's to a friend or a neighbor looking to make a few extra bucks or someone overseas. The best part is you usually don't have to pay a fixed monthly fee for their equipment or their overhead; you are only paying for the service they provide to your business when you need it. You may pay a little more on an hourly basis than you would for someone working full time in your office but you are only paying for the service when you need it. If the workload is slow, they aren't sitting in a cubicle, chewing gum or surfing the Web and exhausting your limited resources."

Another positive side is that this new kind of business structure also allows you more freedom because you don't have to be in your office at the same time every day to make sure your employees are doing what they are supposed to be doing. But Nanton said, "You do have to be more organized, because you have to be very specific with your wants and needs, which usually forces you to write a detailed plan for the task and then you must determine how much you are willing to pay for the task to be completed. Then you can outsource the job to someone who is willing to do it. There are some great places to find people you can outsource work to. One of my favorites is called 'e-lance,' (www.elance.com) a site for freelancers. You can post a job on the site for just about anything, and then other people bid on the job. Much like eBay, there is a feedback system, you can pay through their system with deposits and they escrow the money until you approve its release. I think everyone should try it out sometime. It may not work for you, but it's worth a shot! Oh, and just remember, the cheapest provider is probably not the one you really want to hire. In many cases, you really do get what you pay for." Another popular service that specializes in overseas labor is www.YourManInIndia.com.

The 4th Power Principle – Positioning Yourself in the Marketplace

Setting up a process so that a budding customer base can find out who you are, what you do and how to contact you is crucial if you expect to nurture and expand your business. Nanton said in order to move forward, you can't be apprehensive about promoting yourself or your commercial potential to the public. "There is a right and a wrong way to successfully promote yourself. I know a lot of real estate agents who think it's appropriate to simply promote their smiling faces, but that kind of promotion actually turns a lot of people off. You have to create a 'buzz,' but you have to do it productively so the public will key in on your message, and, most importantly, you have to actually have a message. It can't be hollow buzz; it must contain real substance.

"You're good at what you do; you've spent a lot of time developing your skills and learning the intricacies of your trade. You've experienced a sequence of events that no one else in the world has ever experienced the same way that you have, and you've taken a particular path to get to the professional level you are at today. You have to learn to embrace the path you've taken, learn from your experiences, figure out what makes you different and promote these factors. It sounds elementary, but most people don't realize that they aren't letting their potential customers and surrounding marketplace know what they're good at and why they are the right choice."

"Every day we see companies in the news that are releasing new products or starting new initiatives. Most people don't realize it, but these companies are actually feeding the media outlets, whether local or national, the news they want people to know about. News editors normally don't go out searching for this information; it is delivered to them through press releases. So, you, as the business owner or manager, can control your own positioning by creating news releases, and it works the same whether you run a large or small business. You can release your news online through a variety of Web sites; I personally like www.prweb.com or www.prlog.com. You should also post your news on your own Web site. Controlling your own news releases allows you to position yourself in any manner and in any direction you desire."

The 5th Power Principle – Control Your Communication -- Don't Let it Control You!

The biggest lie of the 21st century is that technology will make your life easier. Our cell phones, BlackBerries and laptop computers that we use everywhere through WiFi connections are taking up more of our time than they probably should. Nanton contends that technology is never going to make your life easier; instead technology will definitely make your life busier. "When I say busier, I don't mean more productive. Most of our day is spent simply doing busy work. We even set daily deadlines and, many times, by the end of the day you probably didn't complete the task. We perceive that we are so busy that most tasks in our lives take a back seat and nothing ever gets done. We've all heard someone say during the day, 'I'm just so busy all day! I get all these emails and phone calls and that kept me so busy I just couldn't get anything done.' Before long we've waited a day, a week, a month or a year without getting anything accomplished. We often don't set aside time to complete the projects we need to finish, and these tasks are usually much more important than most of the emails we get caught up in responding to.

"When someone owns a business, of course, they want to make their clients happy. But in order to keep a consistent level of customer support, that will follow us no matter how busy we get, we need to set boundaries of when we answer the phone and when we respond to emails. Your clients pay you a fee to do a job for them, and chances are you have more than one client. You need to communicate efficiently with each one, but don't get caught up in bad habits like responding instantly to every single email. This becomes unmanageable when you have more than a handful of clients. If you constantly respond to inquiries, you will find that you have less time to actually do the paying work you've been hired to do. You need to be able to devote your full time and attention to each client's project and not be constantly distracted. Tell clients how you work up front, so their expectations will be met, kindly ask them to leave a message and assure them that you will be professional about calling them back. Let your customers know that if it's an emergency, they are welcome to call your cell phone. But set your personal boundaries because if you don't remove yourself from the hustle and bustle of simply being busy, you'll never accomplish anything. You have to take a break from the BlackBerry or the cell phone now and then otherwise you feel like you're working 24 hours a day."

Nanton explained that it sounds silly, and we all deny that we fall into this category, but we can't forget the fact that we also have personal lives that must be balanced with our day-to-day professional responsibilities. "Someone recently asked me how I balance everything I have going on in my life. I will tell you it is a constant struggle for me but using these tactics helps immensely. If I just 'stay busy' it looks like I'm doing a ton of work, but I might be completing a quarter of the work I'm capable of accomplishing. We have to understand that while email is a revolutionary tool, it can also be dangerous to our productivity. It is a great tool for certain situations, but for most of us it has become more of a distraction than a productive way of communicating. We have all written a 30-minute email response that should have been condensed to say, 'Thanks for the invitation but I can't make it this time,' but instead we get wrapped up in trying to communicate through email and trying to get our tone across, but that is no easy task. Everyone reads things based on the mood they are in when it comes across their desk. If we would have just picked up the phone, we would have had much less risk of hurting the other person's feelings and it would have taken us 1/10 of the time it took to draft a long, drawn-out email. It seems to be a foreign concept these days, but sometimes you should just pick up the phone. If you analyze your communications to make sure you are being as effective as possible, you may find that, in the right situations, if you pick up the phone rather than fire off an email you will find more time to do other things. And that's just one small example. The key here is to analyze your communication and make proactive decisions to control it, rather than letting it control you."

The 6th Power Principle – Get Accountable

In order to become an effective and objective business person in today's 21st-century commercial climate, you must take responsibility for the things that occur in your life, good or bad. Nanton believes the best way to get accountable to yourself and your business is to become accountable to others. "I really advocate joining or creating a group of like-minded individuals who are in a similar industry or are looking to forge ahead and receive more rewards in their business life. Set up monthly group meetings with people who are targeting the same goals in their life as you are. Brainstorm and discuss the projects you are working on. You'll soon find out that when you outwardly share your goals with your peers one month, if you show up at the next meeting without accomplishing your objectives, you'll not only feel like you let yourself down, but you'll also feel like you let the members of your accountability group down. This type of environment creates a healthy kind of peer pressure and a sense of camaraderie that forces you to get things done.

Find people who you enjoy being with, and that you don't mind sharing information with, and make yourself accountable to them; it's a great way to motivate yourself because you'll be anxious to get to the next meeting to let everyone know what you've accomplished. This is a really great way to accelerate your success."

The 7th Power Principle – Sell Information

In today's business world, everyone has the opportunity to become an expert because everyone has a certain amount of specialized information in their head. Nanton said that when we talk about other concepts of scalability and positioning, it ties into the fact that if you can take your information and turn it into something tangible, like a written newsletter or a compact disk, you can sell it or use it as a tool to gain new customers. Nanton explained, "Let's take another example, a personal trainer. This is a great way to prospect and a great way to make some extra money. If the personal trainer is really getting better results for their clients in half the time, they've probably created a system for accomplishing this. While the system may not be anything completely new, or it may be a combination of other systems, if this trainer can find a way to put their "spin" on it, they will reach a group of people that most likely no one else has reached before. We all connect with different types of people, and there is room for more personalities in the marketplace because you just don't know who is ready to learn from someone like you, and after all there is only one "you." Instead of just keeping this system in the trainer's head and making money implementing it for clients, why not write down the system, include all the collateral materials that they're using, including marketing materials, client intake forms, client progress reports, workout summaries and anything else they've created and then sell that system to other personal trainers. At that point, not only is the personal trainer a business-to-consumer solution, but now the trainer has figured out a way to become a valuable source of information for other businesses as well. He has added a business to business component. Not to mention that you could sell a version of this product to consumers as well who would rather work out on their own, without the added cost of a trainer. Using this strategy you can instantly create another income stream."

Nanton explained that you can make money by selling your informational system or by giving pieces of it away to prospective clients to show them your level of knowledge and competency. At that point, you become the expert in your field. "People always ask me, 'How does someone become an expert?' And the true response is -- you tell people you're an expert. Even more powerful is if you can get other people to tell everyone you're an expert, and you can do this through the use of third-party testimonials. Another great vehicle to becoming an expert is to write a book on a chosen topic. If you write a book and someone has taken the time to read it, then you've got a great opportunity to gain a customer; it is as if you just spent hour after hour speaking directly to them. By this time they've certainly connected with you and decided whether they like you or not and to them you are the expert from that moment on."

The 8th Power Principle – Breakthroughs

Now that you've started from scratch, developed your tools, understood the concepts of effective communications, written your book and joined the necessary support groups in the local area, the next step is to reap the harvest of what you've created. Nanton said we all want as many "breakthroughs" as possible for our businesses because that's where we make money. "You've learned your whole life that you must first go to first grade, then to second grade, and that you just need to take things one step at a time. Well, while you still have to go through grade school that way for the most part, I'm here to tell you that in the real world that's a lie! Don't believe it. What you should do is take massive action. Let's say you want to start implementing some of these steps; don't take them one at a time – do them all! You won't be great at all of them at first, but if you start working on all eight of these Power Principles simultaneously, it will come together much faster. If you start working on one principle a month for eight months, think about how long it will take you before you can start making things happen. That's how you create breakthroughs while your profit potential begins to grow exponentially. Keep in mind, you must stay focused."

Begin developing a lifestyle versus a "workstyle." Nanton stressed, "Massive action is what makes this system work. If you plan to send out a postcard soliciting business from new clients, try multiple different versions to see which one works best. Massive action produces breakthroughs. If you only send out one copy or one version, you'll never know whether it was great or not."

If you own a business, of course, you want it to be profitable. The difference between a great company and a good company can be measured through solid innovative thinking, a positive attitude and the passion to make a difference in your niche. You have to actively participate to make things happen. Nanton ended on an extremely realistic note, "Not all of these principles will work in every business, and some things won't always work the first time you try them. Have backup plans, create a cash reserve and try to set up something you know is consistent. However, if you're up for the challenge, take massive action using these Power Principles for 30 days in a row. I bet you will see an increase in your income, and at the very worst you will learn a few lessons along the way about what works and what doesn't. Remember, there is risk in everything, but without risk there is no reward."

Most importantly, have faith in yourself. You got into business because you trusted your gut, and you know you are good at what you do. Never second guess yourself on that point and keep pressing on because quite often the most successful businessman is simply the most persistent.

ACKNOWLEDGEMENTS

There are many people who contribute to what an author finally puts down on paper, and I have been fortunate to know people who are always willing to share ideas that they believe set one business apart from another.

What appears in this book as my ideas have really come from friends, mentors and business associates who shared and conveyed the vision that it is a "person" who can truly give life to a product or service. David Edmunds, my father-in-law, was one of the first, teaching me a simple lesson about putting your picture and personal information on a special folded business card he designed for his real estate salesmen. He thought the personal touch was so important he actually bought his own printing press and made personalized stationary for each of his salesmen with their photos on it. This was a very important idea to him because it was 36 years ago, and you couldn't just run down to your local Kinko's and get it done. It took time and extra money, but he knew it made a difference because it helped people "remember you, and you stand apart when they see your picture" he always said.

David's idea was not my last lesson about the importance of developing yourself as a personality for your product or service, and each time I forgot to do so it cost me money. Over the years, I have spent tens of millions of dollars proving this idea, and I hope this book can save you from learning the lesson the expensive way and allow you to make money faster.

The media has changed over the years, and I have to thank James Dicks, Nick Nanton, Lindsay Glass and Jennifer Burg for bringing me into the modern age of SEO marketing, blogs, wikis, Facebook and MySpace. They have shown me how old and proven ideas can be brought up-to-date and capitalized on. And that…is another lesson we may write about someday.

~ Jack

I would like to thank my Lord and Savior, Jesus Christ, through whom all things (including this book) are possible. Thank you for your love and guidance.

Kristina, my wife, partner and best friend, for listening to my crazy ideas all the time and not sending me to the loony bin. I love you and could not do any of the things I do without your support. Thanks for not giving up on me and making me realize that the best things in life are often standing right in front of you begging you to notice them. You are a beautiful person inside and out, and I'm always proud to have you on my arm. Also, I can never thank you enough for our two little boys. The party is just beginning!

Brock and Bowen, although you are still in the earliest portion of your lives, I'm more proud of you than anything I've ever created in my entire life, and I can't wait for you both to show the world what you've got to offer (and if its anything like the blue eyes you have both been blessed with, look out world!). I love you both dearly and can't wait to spend lots of time showing you both how to live, laugh and love, and hope I can be half the parent that my parents were to me.

Mum and Dad, wow, where to begin, you have both always been my biggest fans and have gone through more with me than I can ever thank you for. The two of you are undoubtedly the two finest human beings that I will ever get a chance to know, and I'm amazingly proud to call you my parents. The mark you are leaving on the people in this world with your unwavering love and dedication as well as your willingness to always "lend a hand, as well as an ear" will transcend all that you could possibly imagine. The two of you single-handedly make the world a better place one day at a time. I love you both dearly and can't thank you enough.

Andy, it's been amazing growing up with you. You've been my role model since I was old enough to know that you were my big brother, and you've always found ways to make me work harder, really think things through and challenge the status quo. Thanks for always being there for me and teaching me some of the most important lessons in life, including the one that has been the key to my happiness, "To be happy in life, you first have to learn to be happy by yourself. Don't look for someone else to come in and fill the void. Become happy with who and what you are, and then someone else can magnify that." Thanks for that advice and your friendship. Krista, thanks for making Andy happy. It's a tough job, but you fit the bill to a T! I am proud of your tenacity and ability to go out and accomplish exactly what you desire and look forward to your long and successful career in interior architecture.

Clint and Amanda, you guys are great family and even more than that you're great friends. Thanks for all that you guys do for us, and I look forward to spending the rest of our lives together. Oh yeah... and Go Gators! (Sorry, I couldn't resist.)

Dr. and Mrs. Brock, thanks for letting your daughter marry a wild man. Both of your love and support is extremely encouraging, and I'm thankful that I married into such a great family.

Kara, thanks for all of your support and thanks for letting me marry your big sister. You are about to enter the best years of your life. Don't let them blow by. Make sure you stop and take the time to enjoy them.

Jack, I can never thank you enough for your willingness to take me under your wing and teach me about business, but more importantly about life. I owe this accomplishment and many others to you. I hope one day to be able to teach someone else a fraction of the lessons you have taught me. Your kindness, generosity and willingness to help never go unnoticed. Thanks for helping me feel like I'm not the only crazy person in this world, now I know there are at least two of us! I look forward to much more success for which I will continue to say, "Thank You."

~ Nick

More Celebrity Branding You™!

Just as those of you who are successful in life and in business know that you can't expect to stay at the top of your industry if you relax once you reach the pinnacle of success, we also know that you will need to stay on top of your Celebrity Branding™ process. In order to make this easy for you we've created www.CelebrityBrandingYou.com for you to keep up with all of the newest tips and strategies that we uncover as we continue to work with some of the biggest and best in the business.

Be sure to visit www.CelebrityBrandingYou.com to sign-up for our free CelebrityZine™ as well as to find many great resources that you can use so you won't be left behind. We look forward to hearing about your success and welcome your correspondence.

We can be reached at:

JW Dicks, Esq.
JWDicks@DicksNanton.com
800-981-1403

Nick Nanton, Esq.
NDNanton@DicksNanton.com
800-981-1403

Here's to the bringing out the Celebrity in You!

Jack & Nick

www.ingramcontent.com/pod-product-compliance
Lightning Source LLC
LaVergne TN
LVHW091636100826
845152LV00005B/66

* 9 7 8 0 6 1 5 1 8 6 9 9 3 *